C000215011

# BUSES AND TRAMS
# OF BATH

*Front cover illustration:*
*Above:*
*Bristol LD6 B L8382 leaves Orange Grove for Twerton on Service 12 on 26th June 1961. New in September 1956, it was owned by Bath Electric Tramways until it was withdrawn in August 1972 and sold for scrap. (P.R. Forsey)*

*Below:*
*The Bath trams remained basically unchanged throughout their 35 years in operation. Tram 11 stands outside the GWR Railway Station when running on the Weston route. The advertisements are of interest. (B.Y. Williams/BVBG)*

*Rear cover illustration:*
*FSF6G 6041 (806 MHW) was received by Bath Electric Tramways in October 1961. It was sold to Western National in August 1967 who allocated it fleet number 1009. It was withdrawn from service in August 1978 and purchased by the author and Euel Lane for preservation in November 1978. Perhaps, to ease traffic congestion in the city more people ought to take notice of the rear advertisement. (S.M. Chislett)*

*8096 (OHY 945) was originally intended for use on Bath's country services but eventually operated in Bath City. Here it turns off the A4 London Road at Stambridge into Coalpit Road and Elmhurst Estate on 26th June 1956, some two months after the introduction of service 3A. Note the large destination display. (P.R. Forsey)*

# BUSES AND TRAMS
# OF BATH

STEVE CHISLETT

Millstream Books

First Published in 1986 by
Millstream Books
7, Orange Grove
Bath, BA1 1LP


© Steve Chislett

ISBN 0948975032

Text set in 12 point Bembo
Typeset by Addkey Print Ltd., Corsham
Printed in Great Britain by
Netherwood Dalton, Bradley Mills, Huddersfield, Yorkshire

All rights reserved. No part of this publication may be
reproduced, stored in a retrieval system, or transmitted, in
any form or by any means, electronic, mechanical, photo-
copying, recording or otherwise, without the prior permission
of Millstream Books.

# CONTENTS

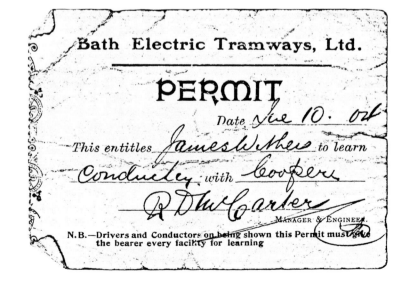

# PREFACE

I had been contemplating for some time the production of an illustrated book dealing with public transport in the City of Bath and was extremely pleased to be asked by Millstream Books to produce this volume. Wherever possible, I have used photographs which have not been previously published, but some have been and are included for their particular interest.

Many people have assisted me in various ways during the preparation of the book and I must particularly thank Phil Forsey of Batheaston, Stan Weston of Warminster and Allan Macfarlane of Bristol for allowing me access to their comprehensive personal photographic collections. Dave Withers and the late Roy Gingell of the Bristol Vintage Bus Group, Robert Mack of Leeds, Mike Tozer of Pill, Peter Davey of Bristol, Martin Curtis of Weymouth and Lionel Tancock of Bath were also of great help in this matter.

Ken Cochrane gave up much time making prints from Phil Forsey's negatives and Chris Carr and Warwick Hulme supplied historical information from Company records.

My wife, Deirdre, was an essential morale booster when spirits sagged and has put up with many months of chaos in the household. My children; Jeremy, Billy, Mary, Anna and Caleb were particularly cooperative in leaving my chaos well alone!

I hope that photographs have been credited correctly as every effort has been made to contact owners for permission to use them. As far as I am aware the text and captions are correct but I apologise for any errors in advance. Please advise me through the publisher of any corrections required.

The content of the book is as varied as circumstances would allow and I trust that there is plenty to satisfy all tastes. I hope that the illustrations and information stimulate an interest in the rapidly changing scene of public transport in Bath and, maybe, rekindle memories of Bath and its transport in less hectic days.

Stephen M. Chislett, Batheaston. September 1986

Bibliography:
The following books were consulted during the compilation of the various chapters:-
The People's Carriage published by Bristol Omnibus Co in 1974.
Tramways of the West of England by P.W. Gentry, published by The Light Railway Transport League in 1960.
Bath Tramways by Colin Maggs, published by Oakwood Press in 1971.
Bristol Omnibus Fleet Histories published by The PSV Circle and The Omnibus Society.
Various Company records, timetables and publicity.

Opposite:
Delivered as L8567 (708 JHY) this FSF6G was renumbered L6009 in January 1961. It was new to Bath Tramways Motor Co in November 1960 and later passed to Bath Electric Tramways in November 1962 and back again to BTM in December 1962! In August 1967 it was sold to Southern National and eventually received NBC red livery and Devon General fleetnames in November 1976. It was withdrawn in February 1978 and sold to a dealer. It was pictured on Old Bridge on 12th October 1960 before it was renumbered. Wansdyke Estate is no longer served by a bus service. (P.R. Forsey)

Below:
Tram 34 is seen here in April 1939 on Old Bridge destined for Devonshire Buildings. Compare this scene with that above. There is no change in the surroundings over 21 years. (J. Luckman/BVBG)

THE
PUBLIC CONVEYANCES
FROM THE
YORK HOUSE, BATH,
Royal Mail Office,
Are constructed upon the most approved
principles of safety.

SHOULD ANY
IRREGULARITIES OCCUR,
IT IS REQUESTED THAT
Immediate Application
BE MADE TO
WILLIAM LANE.

# ROYAL MAIL AND GENERAL COACH OFFICE,

# YORK HOUSE, BATH.

## Royal Mails.

**LONDON**—through Devizes, Marlborough, and Reading, every Evening at a quarter past Seven.

**LONDON**—through Chippenham and Calne, every Evening at Eight.

**EXETER**—through Wells, Bridgewater, and Taunton, every Morning at Seven.

**PLYMOUTH and DEVONPORT direct**—through Totness, every Morning at Seven, and arrives the same Evening at half-past Nine.

**FALMOUTH**—through Truro and Launceston, every Morning at Seven.

**BARNSTAPLE and ILFRACOMBE** through Wiveliscombe and South Molton, every Morning at a-quarter before Seven.

**PORTSMOUTH** *(New Mail)*—through Warminster, Salisbury, and Southampton, every Evening at a quarter past Eight.

**CHELTENHAM** — through Tetbury and Cirencester, every Afternoon at half-past Two.

**BIRMINGHAM MANCHESTER,** through Gloucester and Worcester, every Afternoon at half-past Four.

**MILFORD, HAVERFORDWEST,** through Swansea and Carmarthen, every Morning at Six.

**BRISTOL and CLIFTON**—every Morning at Five and Six, and Afternoon at Three and half-past Four.

## Post Coaches.

**LONDON,** *(York House Day Coach),* in 11 hours, through Chippenham, Marlborough, and Reading, every Morning at Seven, to the Gloucester Coffee House, Piccadilly, and Belle Sauvage, Ludgate Hill.

**LONDON,** *(Regulator),* in 11 hours, same route, every Morning at half-past Eight, to the Hatchett's Hotel, Piccadilly, and Bull and Mouth, St. Martin's le Grand.

**LONDON,** *(Emerald),* in 11 hours, through Devizes, every Morning at half-past Nine, to the Gloucester Coffee House, Piccadilly, and Spread Eagle, Grace-church-street. No Fees.

**LONDON,** *(Monarch),* through Chippenham and Calne, every Evening, at Seven, to the Hatchett's Hotel, Piccadilly, and Belle Sauvage, Ludgate Hill. No Fees.

**READING,** *(Star),* through Devizes, Marlborough, and Newbury, every Morning (except Sunday), at Ten.

**EXETER,** *(Retaliator),* through Wells, Glastonbury, Somerton, Langport, Ilminster, and Honiton, every Morning (except Sunday), at half-past Eight.

**SIDMOUTH,** every Morning at a-quarter past Eight.

**LYME,** through Shepton Mallet, Ilchester, and Axminster, Monday, Wednesday, and Friday Mornings, at Eight.

**PLYMOUTH AND DEVONPORT,** through Chudleigh, every Morning, (Sunday excepted) at half past 8.

**SOUTHAMPTON,** *(Rocket),* through Warminster, Salisbury, and Romsey, Monday, Wednesday and Friday Mornings, at Eight.

**BIRMINGHAM,** *(York House Coach),* through Stroud. Painswick, and Tewkesbury, every Morning, (except Sunday), at Eight.

**CHELTENHAM, WORCESTER, and SHREWSBURY,** every Morning, (except Sunday), at a quarter before Eight.

**BRIGHTON,** *(Red Rover),* in 13 hours, through Warminster, Salisbury, Southampton, Chichester, Arundell, and Worthing, Tuesday, Thursday, and Saturday Mornings, at Eight.

*The Red Rover is the only Coach that arrives at Southampton in time for the Steam Packets to Cowes, Ryde, &c.*

**PORTSMOUTH AND GOSPORT,** every Morning (except Sunday), at Eight.

**WARWICK, LEAMINGTON, AND COVENTRY,** every Morning (except Sunday), at Eight.

**LIVERPOOL,** every Morning (Sunday excepted), at a quarter before Eight, and Afternoon at half-past Four.

**WEYMOUTH,** *(Wellington)* through Frome, Bruton, Sherborne, and Dorchester, Monday, Wednesday, and Friday Mornings, at half-past Eight.

*This Coach arrives in time for the Government Steam Packet to Jersey, Guernsey, &c.*

**OXFORD,** *(Oxonian)* through Chippenham, Swindon, and Farringdon, every Monday, Wednesday, and Friday Mornings, at half-past Eight.

**MANCHESTER, CARLISLE, and EDINBURGH,** every Morning, (except Sunday), at a quarter before Eight.

**CHESTER AND HOLYHEAD,** every Morning, (except Sunday), at Eight, and Afternoon at half-past Two.

**OXFORD,** *(Collegian)* through Tetbury & Cirencester, every Morning (Sunday excepted), at Nine.

**DEVIZES,** every Afternoon, (except Sunday), at a quarter past Five.

**WESTON - SUPER - MARE AND CLEVEDON,** *(Sovereign)* every Morning at half-past Seven.

**CLIFTON,** every Morning at a quarter before Ten, and Afternoon at Three.

**BRISTOL,** Coaches every hour.

*Every Information may be obtained at this Office relative to the Steam Packets to Ireland, South Wales, &c.*

**WILLIAM LANE, Proprietor.**

# CHAPTER 1 – EVERYTHING IS HORSEDRAWN

Stage coaches, which were introduced in the middle of the seventeenth century, heralded the first real type of public transport. But this style of travel left much to be desired as journeys were often late, particularly in the winter months, and were renowned for discomfort. In fact the services advertised could be described as fair weather services, in that heavy or continuous rain or snow often resulted in the suspension of the journeys until the mud roads had dried out sufficiently to support the carriages. The fares charged were very expensive and, therefore, beyond the means of most people.

Many of the roads were littered with debris and large stones causing carriages to sway, which frequently resulted in the passengers suffering from stomach nausea similar to sea-sickness. Most of these stage coaches were nicknamed hellcarts as, initially, there were no windows but merely openings which were boarded up during inclement weather. Glazing for stage coaches and carriages in general became common from about 1710 and undoubtedly improved travelling conditions, whatever the time of year.

By the middle of the eighteenth century, road surfaces on the main routes had been improved to such an extent that passengers endured a far more comfortable passage with much increased safety. The only other main peril, however, that of the highwaymen, remained a constant problem, although it was hoped that the blunderbuss supplied to the coachman was a deterrent to the would-be thieves.

What was considered as the ultimate perfection in coach travel occurred on Monday 2nd August 1784 when the first mail services in the country were introduced between Bristol and London via Bath. These services were introduced by John Palmer of Bath, in agreement with the Postmaster General to King George III, to carry the mails of the country and were distinguished from the stage carriage services by the armed guard employed by the Government. The stage coaches had taken from Monday night until the next Wednesday afternoon to complete the 103 miles between Bath and London. The mail coach in 1830, however, was advertised as follows: "Flying machines to London in one day! From the beginning of April to Michaelmas. Set out from the White Lion in the Market Place and White Hart in Stall Street, every night at eleven o'clock, and arrive in London the next evening. Passengers to pay one pound eight shillings each".

The result of the better journey time was a large increase in the number of passengers who were now being protected to a certain extent by both the coachman and guard being armed against the highwaymen. The next mail coach service was introduced in March 1785 between London and Norwich and in May between Bristol and Portsmouth. The popularity of the mail coach was causing concern for the stage coach owners until the railways began to oust both stage and mail coaches as the preferred method of travel for longer distances.

In 1827 and 1828 a gentleman named Goldsworthy Gurney constructed a 6-wheeled, 3-axled, steam-powered coach which could accommodate 18 seated passengers. His ill-fated trial journey started on 28th July 1829 when he left London and planned to travel to Bath by way of Calne, Melksham and Bradford-on-Avon. He had failed to note, however, that it was fair day in Melksham and was met by a particularly hostile crowd of villagers who swarmed around the coach shouting "Down with all machinery". Then they threw stones and bricks at the coach, damaged the engine and seriously injured several of the passengers. Following the riot, Gurney continued to Bath, a mere 12¼ miles from Melksham, where repairs took 2 days to complete and, no doubt, gave him sufficient time to ponder over the high cost of his oversight! On his return from Bath to London a few mechanical problems occurred which resulted in the 84 miles from Melksham to Cranford Bridge taking 10 hours to complete. Development of the steam carriage for road transport was severely jeopardised after these initial experiments by the enthusiastic advancement of passenger railway lines throughout Britain.

Many timetables of Royal Mail and Post Coaches were published by the owners of stage coaches and coaching inns. The undated example on page 8 details departures from the Royal Mail and General Coaching Office, York House, Bath to various towns and cities by Royal Mail coach.

Mail and Stage coaches were eventually withdrawn between Bath and London in 1841 because of competition from the railways. The last regular mail coach to operate was between Wick and Thurso which was withdrawn in 1874 due to competition from the Highland Railway.

Horse omnibuses operating local journeys were first introduced by George Shillibeer in London in 1829 and the idea was quickly copied in many other British cities and towns. Scheduled horse-drawn local public transport was well established in Bath and the surrounding villages by the mid-1870s. These were invariably operated with converted farm wagons owned by local hauliers or farmers to raise additional income. Purpose-built horse bus bodies became a common sight during the 1880s and 1890s and the Bath Road Car and Tramway Company timetable for November 1895 shows that horse bus routes were operated from Bond Street to Twerton, Fairfield Park, Prior Park Road, Lower Weston, Upper Weston, Bathford, Larkhall, Oldfield Park, Devonshire Arms and Combe Down on frequent or reasonably frequent timetables. A twice daily service was also run between Bond Street and Newton St. Loe and there was at times a limited amount of cross-city working via Bond Street. This resulted in such journeys as Twerton to Larkhall,

Fairfield Park to Prior Park Road or Lower Weston; Lower Weston to Larkhall; and Devonshire Arms to Larkhall. The specific reasons for these particular journeys is not known and in some instances there was no corresponding return facility.

In addition to the horse bus routes, a horse-drawn tram service was operated between Grosvenor and the GWR Station and ran every 15 minutes. Additional late journeys were scheduled to operate on Saturdays on all services except the tram route and the bus routes to Prior Park Road, Newton, Devonshire Arms and Combe Down.

*Horse Tramcar 2 operated by Bath Road Car & Tramway Co Ltd is seen outside St James's Church sometime in the 1880s. The church was blitzed in the Second World War. (Photo reproduced by courtesy of Bath Evening Chronicle)*

Plans for a horse tramway in Bath were originally lodged in September 1878 with proposed routes between the top of Broad Street and Lambridge and another linking the GWR and Midland railway stations. In 1879, however, a larger plan for routes between Batheaston and Twerton and from the city to Combe Down, Lansdown and Weston were submitted but Bath Corporation accepted the proposals from Bristol Tramways Company Ltd for a route from Grosvenor to the GWR Station with a depot alongside the Porter Butt Inn on London Road. It was originally hoped to operate this route along Pierrepont Street but objectors forced the Company to change its plans and operate the service via Southgate Street.

Bath Tramways Company Ltd was then formed in July 1880 with a capital of £50,000 in £10 shares and work on laying the track started by 22nd September 1880 in Walcot Street. Various streets were closed to expedite this work which was carried out by Augustus Krauss of Bristol and was completed in time for an official inspection of the route to be carried out by a Major General Hutchinson, for the Board of Trade, on 23rd December 1880. The following day the tramway was officially opened by the Mayor, accompanied by many members of the Corporation, who rode from the GWR Station to Grosvenor and returned for a luncheon at the Grand Pump Room Hotel in Stall Street.

*The staff proudly stand in front of one of the Horse Tramcars outside the Porter Butt Inn on 5th September 1881. The depot was in the yard adjacent to the inn. (Bristol Vintage Bus Group)*

*Henry Gould's Horse Bus which operated between Twerton and Larkhall. The message painted onto the stair panel is of particular interest. (Jack Bishop collection)*

The Company suffered from poor patronage and low receipts which led to the abandonment of a plan to extend the line to Twerton. A reduction in the fare between New Bond Street and the GWR Station merely resulted in a reduction in receipts up to September 1882, and the introduction of a parcels service was not as successful as had been hoped. Receipts, however, between September 1882 and March 1883 increased sufficiently to allow payment of some outstanding interests. Despite this, the financial state of the Company was so poor that the Secretary and Directors received no pay during 1883, saving a total of £100. A typical report in the Bath Chronicle of 29th December 1885 stated "Bath Tramways – For the week ending 25th December, the total receipts were £53.11s.9d. and the passengers carried 7,949".

*Horse Bus No 15 owned by The Bath Road Car & Tramways Co Ltd is seen outside the Crown & Anchor Inn, Weston during the 1880s. The young conductor and advertisements are characteristic of the period. (M.J. Tozer collection)*

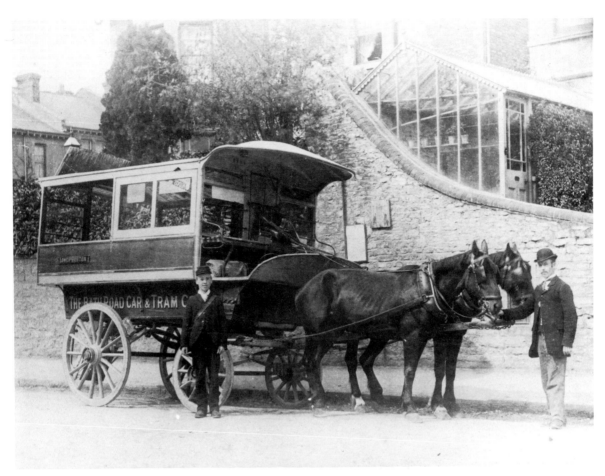

*The board on the body of the Horse Bus reads Lower Weston, and the photograph was taken at Rosslyn Road during the 1880s. The gentleman holding the reins is Henry Fowler, who was known as Harry, accompanied by a particularly young looking conductor. (A. Bland)*

The City Council met the Company's Secretary, George White, on 11th March 1884 when White requested that the Corporation buy the horses and rolling stock but the Council officers were unhappy about the proposal. White was successful in securing an agreement with the Patent Cable Tramways Corporation whereby they would purchase the tramway and at a meeting held on 8th May 1884 the shareholders agreed unanimously to the sale.

Unfortunately, the new Company was no luckier than the original owners and on 11th August 1888 the Company was sold again to Dick, Kerr and Company. In 1886 the Bath Omnibus Road Car Company Ltd had been formed to purchase and run the horse bus and carriage businesses of Henry Gould, who operated to Weston and Twerton, and Frederick Lavington, who operated services to Batheaston and Bathford. On 1st April 1889 their interest turned to the tramway when it was purchased from Dick, Kerr for £5,500 and the Company was renamed Bath Road Car and Tramways Company Ltd. In the first three months of tram operation this latest Company announced that receipts had increased quite substantially. The winter of 1891

was extremely hard and the trams and buses were prevented from operating on numerous occasions. Snow clearance had cost £500 and receipts had been badly affected by the inability to run the advertised routes. Although the Company's performance varied from year to year, overall it was able to pay dividends to all interested parties.

In 1902 the tramway was purchased for £5,210 by Bath Corporation on behalf of Bath Electric Tramways. The price paid was settled only after arbitration by Sir Frederick Bramwell, and Bath Electric Tramways subsequently received £446.13s.3d. from the sale of the rolling stock, horses and office equipment.

On 25th July 1902 the last horse tram operated and carried Councillor Tuckett who had also travelled on board the first car on the opening day. A horse bus service was operated between Larkhall and the GWR Station via the Paragon and Milsom Street to replace the trams and, on 27th August 1902, the Company's name was changed to Bath Carriage and Omnibus Ltd. The revised Company continued to run horse buses until 19th February 1904 when the competing electric trams caused it to go into liquidation.

The horse tram route involved 2 inclines which it was felt required an additional horse, known as a trace horse, to assist the car up the hill. These were used between the Bell Inn and the top of Walcot Street and between Walcot Parade and the top of Walcot Street. The same trace horse would usually assist a car up from the Bell and then be walked down to Walcot Parade to assist a car approaching from Grosvenor.

Originally 6 single-deck cars were purchased from George Starbuck of Birkenhead and seated 18 passengers. In 1884 when the Patent Cable Company took over, an additional 7 single-deck cars seating 12 passengers were bought. Until about 1899 the trams ran every 10 minutes but after this the frequency was reduced to every 15 minutes. The first departure from Grosvenor was at 08.30 and the last at 22.30 on Mondays to Saturdays and at 14.00 and 22.00 on Sundays. From the GWR Station the corresponding journeys on Mondays to Saturdays were at 09.15 and 23.00 but, because trams were not allowed along Dorchester Street on Sundays, the city departures were from Old Bridge between 14.30 and 22.30.

*Harry Fowler is again seen in this view taken in 1902 wearing a white hat and whistle. Horse Bus 52 is on the Bathford route. (A. Bland)*

# CHAPTER 2 – ELECTRIC TRAMS

The use of electric trams as a method of local travel was well advanced in towns and cities throughout Britain by 1900 and the operation of an electric tramway in Bath was a popular idea which led to many plans and submissions from interested parties. Suggestions that an electric tramway be operated in the city were first aired in 1898 when the Corporation was informed by British Electric Traction and British Finance and Investment Company of their interests in the subject. However, the Corporation wished to ensure that any such transport system should be controlled by them and consequently on 17th December 1898 an Electric Traction Joint Committee was formed to consider and investigate the matter.

In 1899 an offer was received from Drake and Gorham Electric Power and Traction Company to build an electric tramway system and in May that year further plans were submitted by Bath and District Light Railways for various routes in the city and certain of the surrounding villages, although these plans were amended in November. The proposals of the latter party included a tram depot in Upper Bristol Road and a power station in Dorchester Street close to the Corporation's own power station.

An offer to electrify the horse tramway and operate routes to Twerton, Lower Weston, Batheaston and Devonshire Buildings was made in early 1900 by British Electric Traction and a rival submission for a similar project was lodged by the Bath Road Car Company. A Light Railway Order application was made jointly by Bath Corporation with Sir James Sivewright and Leopold Hirsch in May 1900 to form Bath and District Light Railways Company Ltd. The intention of this Company was to operate routes from Bath GWR Station to Bathford (New Inn), Newbridge Park, Weston, Twerton, Oldfield Park and Combe

*It is believed that this photograph was taken in 1902 when the lines were being laid for the operation of electric trams. The site is near the Green Park Tavern. (G. Drew)*

9. — BATH. — G. W. Railway Station and Station Hotel. — LL.

Single Deck Tram 52 heads towards the Guildhall terminus with the destination blind set for the return journey to Oldfield Park amid an abundance of horsedrawn vehicles. Note the footbridge between the Royal Station

*The trams were garaged at Walcot Street in a purpose built depot which survives today albeit slightly altered. Seven trams are lined up for service, from the left – Nos 4, 32, 16, 14, 1, 50 and 22 on 18th April 1938. (W.A. Camwell)*

Down (Convalescent Home). This scheme was to be built to the most common gauge of 4 feet 8½ inches with a Company capital of £225,000 in £1 shares. The proposal received the Board of Trade Light Railway Order approval on 2nd November 1901.

Bath and District Light Railways Company was transferred in April 1903 to Bath Electric Tramways Ltd which had been formed on 9th July 1902. Proposals for additional routes and abandonment of certain other sections by the new Company included the need for a new bridge across the river, which resulted in the construction of Midland Bridge for which the Company contributed two thirds of the cost. The bridge, however, was never used as a tram route because the Company was prohibited from using Westgate Street for operating trams and the sum of £8,400 paid by the Company was forfeited.

Construction of the tramway lines began in November 1902 under the provisions of the Light Railways Act 1896 and started in Walcot Street. The work was carried out by Charles Chadwell of London who paid 4½d (approximately 2p) an hour to the men working a 12-hour day. The construction of the overhead wiring was also contracted to Chadwell but

the contract for building the depot, generating station and completion of the tramcars was awarded to British Westinghouse Electrical and Manufacturing Company. Additional expense was incurred by the Company during 1903 when it was found necessary to realign tramlines outside the Guildhall and the Roman Baths in Stall Street to accommodate stand room for carriages. London Street had to be closed to enable the tram lines to be laid in the road surface but when it was later discovered that the lines were not laid evenly or to the correct levels, it was necessary to free Cleveland Bridge from charging tolls for traffic which had been diverted because of these irregularities. The suspension of tolls in March 1903 resulted in the bridge owners being paid £35 for the first week and £30 on subsequent weeks, this amount being met equally by the contractors and the Corporation.

It had been intended to begin operation of the services in November 1903 but as the power station at Walcot Depot was incomplete this was not possible. The tramcars were, however, delivered in early December and were completed at the Walcot Street depot whilst the depot itself was still being connected to Walcot Street. The Board of Trade inspection was

*Passengers could transfer from tram to bus and vice-versa at Bathford, Glasshouse and Newton St Loe. Tram 28 is seen at Bathford Bridge where certain passengers are transferring to a Milnes Daimler bus registration FB 05. (M.J. Tozer collection)*

*Tram 23 stands outside the GWR Station and Royal Hotel on 18th April 1938. The footbridge had been removed by this time. (W.A. Camwell)*

*Conductor W. Ransom and Motorman G. White with Tram 15 at Twerton terminus in July 1932. (S.M. Chislett collection)*

scheduled to be carried out by Colonel Von Donop, a Bathonian, on 12th December 1903 at 09.45, by travelling over the routes by tram from the Guildhall. Unfortunately, a power station failure prevented the arrival of the trams and it was decided to inspect part of the system by carriage and pairs which duly departed the Guildhall at 10.30. Later that day, however, the fault was rectified and the whole system was covered by tramcar by the Colonel and the other officers.

Tram drivers, known as motormen, were initially recruited from other areas of the country to operate the trams but, later, conductors were trained as motormen by the Company itself when they were promoted. Conductors undergoing driving training did so during their own time, were not paid and after a lengthy training period were tested by the Chief Inspector in the practical and written aspects of the work.

The passenger service commenced at 11.00 on 2nd January 1904 when the first double-deck tram departed for Bathford followed by trams on the other routes. As only 2 of the 6 single-deck trams had been delivered to the Company by this date, the route to Oldfield Park did not begin until 23rd January. Even then the route was operated using the 2 single-deck

*Tram No 6 was decorated to publicise the Mayor's Distress Fund in February 1923 and is seen in the depot yard. (Jack Bishop collection)*

*Tram 8 is seen on 18th April 1938 at the Bathford terminus by the Crown Inn at the bottom of Bathford Hill. Note the passengers boarding and alighting from the tram in the middle of the road. (W.A. Camwell)*

trams available and then only between the GWR Station and Oldfield Park. From 14th July 1904, however, the city terminal point was extended to the Guildhall following the completion of the Manvers Street and Pierrepont Street line which then enabled one-way working of services via these roads on journeys going northward, and via Cheap Street, Stall Street and Southgate Street on journeys southward from the depot and the Guildhall. Approximately 22,800 passengers were carried on the first day despite a few teething problems which rendered some of the tramcars unavailable for service. The temporary terminus of the Combe Down service at Devonshire Arms was extended to the Workhouse (later St. Martin's Hospital) in Midford Road and was again extended to Combe Down (Convalescent Home) on 31st July 1904, thus replacing the horse bus service between the Workhouse and Combe Down. The official opening of the system by Lady Caillard, wife of Sir Vincent Caillard, Chairman of British Electric Traction, took place on 13th February 1904 with a ceremony at the depot followed by lunch at the

Guildhall. The full extent of the system, a total of 14.78 miles, was completed when an extension of line from Newbridge Park to Newton St. Loe was opened for passenger traffic on 5th August 1905. The extension cost £11,300 but in the first week carried 9,000 passengers who paid £683 in fares and plans were in hand, and granted a Light Railway Order, to extend even further afield to Saltford. Poor receipts due to bad weather and a resulting low number of passengers, however, led to the shelving of this plan. If this extension had been built it is quite probable that the Bath and Bristol tramway systems would have been linked at Saltford or Keynsham and resulted in through operation of trams between the two cities.

The First World War resulted in conductresses being employed from October 1915, to replace the men who had joined the forces, and in December of that year tram drivers were issued with long point bars to avoid conductresses having to alight from the tram to alter the points. From September 1916 women commenced training for driving duties and were allocated to operate trams on the flatter routes such as Twerton

*Tram 12 waits departure time from the terminus at Weston. The scene today is basically unchanged around the War Memorial and church but the advertisements on the shop are just a memory. 18th April 1838. (W.A. Camwell)*

*Tram 12 again! This time at the Newton St Loe terminus at the Globe Inn in 1935. This site is now an extremely busy junction. (S.G. Jackman – Courtesy Bath Reference Library)*

*Tram 14 appears to be waiting for its crew in Northgate Street on its way to Combe Down on 10th September 1937. (H.B. Priestley)*

*A side profile of a double-deck tram at Walcot Street Depot showing the magnetic brake on the track and detail of the body. The advertisements on the decency panels and the small opening windows are of interest. (Bristol Vintage Bus Group)*

*Harry Fowler at the controls of Tram 33 at Newton St Loe terminus in the early years of electric trams before the destination boxes were lowered to the upper deck rail. The conductor is also particularly well turned out. (A. Bland)*

*The rural atmosphere of the Combe Down terminus makes a perfect background for Tram 33 on 18th April 1938. (W.A. Camwell)*

*Tram 15 arriving at the terminal stop outside the Abbey for the Twerton route. It has just operated the wrong way around the roundabout, before June 1937. (W.S. Eade*

or Weston, although they could sometimes also be found on the Combe Down to Bathford runs. On the return of peace the conductresses were replaced by the men returning from the forces and those men who had been recruited as drivers during the war had the choice of returning to conducting duties or leaving the Company.

The operation of the tramway had been maintained by the tramcars originally purchased by the Company between 1903 and 1905 from G.F. Milnes of Birkenhead on trucks manufactured by W.C.F. Busch of Bautzen in Saxony in Germany. The trucks were built to Milnes' specifications and consisted of 34 double-deck cars (numbered 1 to 34) and 6 single-deck cars (numbered 50 to 55), all completed by Milnes. In addition there was a combined water car and track cleaner which was equipped with brushes at each end and was operated to dampen the dusty road conditions

and help prevent tar running into the rail grooves when necessary. The double-deck cars were open-top, balcony type and were unvestibuled (open platform) with half-turn stairs at each end. The single-deck cars were needed to operate under the low railway bridge at the junction of Lower Oldfield Park and Lower Bristol Road at the Green Tree Inn but could be found on other routes when circumstances demanded, particularly on the Bathford and Combe Down routes on Sundays and Bank Holidays. It can be assumed that the vacant numbers between 35 and 49 were for an increase in fleet size for the proposed extension to Saltford or Keynsham.

The seating capacity on the double-decks was 55, with 33 upstairs and 22 downstairs; and on single-decks was 30, with 16 inside and 7 outside at each end. The seats upstairs were of the traditional wooden transverse type with tip-over backs to suit direction of travel and the interior longitudinal bench seating, originally upholstered, was later replaced by the standard slatted polished wood. Despite the seating accommodation it was not uncommon to carry passengers far in excess of the number of seats and it has been reported that over 120 were carried on the last double-deck tram to Bathford one night and 90 passengers on a single-deck car!

Most of the overhead wiring was supported by single side-poles with bracket arms which measured anything from 6 feet to 28 feet in length but in some city centre streets span wires were used, fixed to buildings by rosettes. Automatic trolley reversers were installed at the termini at Bathford, Combe Down, Oldfield Park, Twerton and Newton St. Loe which

dispensed with the need to turn the trolley pole at these sites. Trolley ropes were fitted to all trams to turn the trolley pole but after about a year the single-deck trams were equipped with long bamboo canes with a hook which were stored along the side panels on the outside of the cars.

There was no incentive for the Company to modernise or update its rolling stock and the tramcars, therefore, remained virtually unchanged during their 34-year life span. This was partly due to the report that the Company's franchise for tramway operation was for a period of 32 years, after which the Corporation could exercise its option to purchase the concern. These rights were surrendered by all the local authorities when the tramways were abandoned. During the 1930s Bristol Tramways and Carriage Company

*Obviously a quiet journey to Bathford as Tram 27 operates against a No Entry road marking sometime before June 1937. The buildings in this scene remain basically unchanged ...day. (W.S. Eades)*

*The Guildhall and Abbey were the main central stops for tram services and Tram 24 stands outside the Guildhall en route for Combe Down from Bathford on 21st August 1938. (M.J. O'Connor – A. Gallop collection)*

*Batheaston High Street is the location for this crowd of inquisitive youngsters and Tram 17. The Lamb & Flag Inn to the left of the tram was demolished some years ago. (Postcard – Jack Bishop collection)*

*Trams 50 and 51 pass on Old Bridge on 10th September 1937. (H.B. Priestley)*

*Bath Abbey forms the backcloth to Tram 52 in 1937. (W.S. Eades)*

sought to expand its operating territory and in 1936 acquired Bath Electric Tramways Ltd and Bath Tramways Motor Company Ltd. At a meeting of the City Council on 27th July 1937 it was announced that the city's tram system was to be replaced by a fleet of motorbuses. This decision reflected the general policy of Bristol Tramways for a rapid abolition of trams in favour of buses. On Saturday 3rd November 1938 the first section of route was abandoned, between Newbridge Road and Newton St. Loe. At 22.55 the last tram, car number 14, departed the GWR Station for Newton St. Loe. On reaching Cross Roads Loop, however, all passengers were transferred to a waiting bus which carried them to their destination. This decision, no doubt, had been made by the Bristol Tramways Company following their experience of 'last tram' journeys on earlier closures of tram services in Bristol itself. This was of little consolation to the crowd which had gathered at the Newton St. Loe terminus to greet the final journey.

The next route to be converted was between the Guildhall and Twerton on Saturday 22nd April 1939. This route was replaced by double-decker buses which operated beyond the tram terminus to find a suitable turning place. The remainder of the system was withdrawn 2 weeks later on Saturday 6th May 1939, when the last trams from each of the remaining terminal points were packed to capacity. The last tram of all to arrive at the Guildhall was number 22 from Combe Down at around midnight. It was met by the Mayor, members of the Corporation, officials and the General Manager of the Company. A large crowd of well over 1,000 people cheered the tram, which displayed SPECIAL on the destination blind, on its final trip to the Walcot Street depot. It was packed with a hundred passengers and – with the Mayor, Captain Adrian Hopkins, at the controls, helped by Inspectors Hale and Smale – the tram slowly made its way on the short trip to the depot. On arrival at Walcot Street, the Mayor switched off the electricity supply that had fed the trams with energy during their lifetime. All the trams were subsequently scrapped, most of the cars being broken up and burnt at a specially laid scrapyard at Midford Road opposite St. Martin's Hospital. The trams which operated the late journeys on the final day were, however, scrapped at the Walcot Street depot.

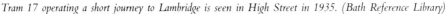

*Tram 17 operating a short journey to Lambridge is seen in High Street in 1935. (Bath Reference Library)*

*Tram 1 operates the last journey from Bathford on Saturday 6th May 1939 when tram services were withdrawn and replaced by motor buses the next day. The occasion was the scene of large crowds at the outer terminus and the Guildhall. The tram is packed to capacity and is passing Lambridge with a load of well wishers on its farewell run. (Reproduced by courtesy of Bath Evening Chronicle)*

*The final arrival at the Guildhall was Tram 22 from Combe Down. The Mayor, Captain Adrian Hopkins, is seen at the controls for the last few hundred yards to Walcot Depot. An abundance of police is present to prevent problems experienced in Bristol where trams were stripped of parts by souvenir hunters. (Reproduced by courtesy of Bath Evening Chronicle)*

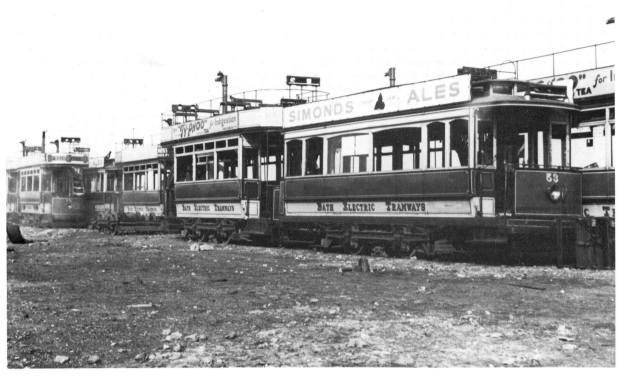

The majority of trams were scrapped at a specially built yard opposite St. Martin's Hospital. Tram 53 is seen at the head of a sad line-up of Bath trams in the scrapyard immediately following the closedown. (S. Miles Davey)

The decorative ironwork, glass and seats have been removed from Tram 33 along with the destination boxes and advertisement panels. Definitely no reprieve – the body will be burnt and the metal salvaged. (S. Miles Davey)

# CHAPTER 3 – MOTORISED BUSES

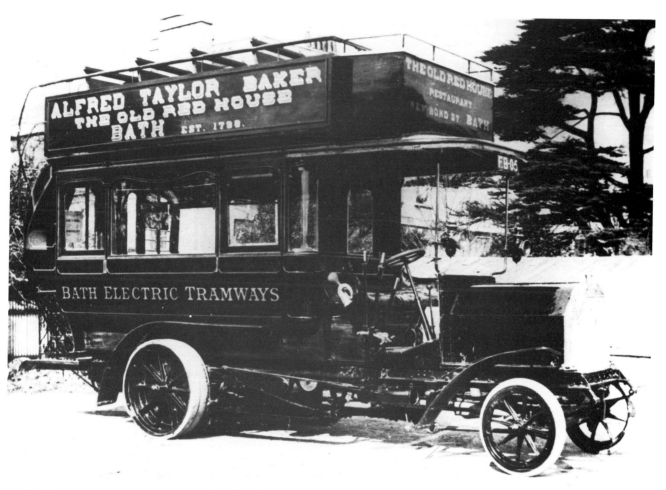

*Six Milnes Daimler double-deck buses were purchased by Bath Electric Tramways in 1905 and FB 05 is seen in the grounds of Kensington Depot. (M.J. Tozer collection)*

The use of motorbuses in Bath had been considered as early as 1900 for routes which were thought to be too steep for the proposed electric tram services. In 1904 Mr. R.D. McCarter, the first General Manager of Bath Electric Tramways Ltd decided to purchase motorbuses to act as feeders to the tramway. To house these vehicles, York Villa and its grounds on the London Road were purchased for £2,200 and the grounds used for garaging the buses, as is the case today. From August 1905, 6 Milnes Daimler and 6 Straker Squires open-top double-deck buses were delivered. The Milnes Daimlers, which seated 32 passengers, were registered FB 02 – FB 07 and cost £7,300 and the Straker Squires, which seated 35 passengers, were registered FB 08 – FB 13 and cost £8,000. They were quickly put to work and rapidly proved their worth, bringing in additional revenue to the tramway by acting as feeders at Glasshouse and Bathford. Bus routes from Glasshouse operated to Frome, Radstock

and Midsomer Norton, and from Bathford (Railway Bridge) to Trowbridge, Devizes and Chippenham.

The Bristol Tramways and Carriage Company was a little slower in adopting motorbuses for its services and did not introduce any until 1906. In February 1907 this Company started operating a motorbus service from the Newton St. Loe tram terminus to Brislington, which at that time was a village outside Bristol, where passengers could transfer to a tram to continue into Bristol. In the late 1920s a further motorbus service was introduced between Bristol and Bath via Hanham, Bitton and Kelston.

The pattern of Bath's tram and bus services continued basically unchanged for many years but the First World War resulted in considerable staffing problems and higher than predicted operating costs. In 1920 capital was required to purchase more buses but because Bath Electric Tramways had not paid dividends to shareholders for many years it was difficult to get

*The crew of single-deck AEC FB 07 proudly prose with their vehicle. Note the Bell Punch on the conductor's strap. (A. Gallop collection)*

*The Straker Squires double-deck buses purchased by Bath Electric Tramways were registered FB 08 – FB 013. FB011 is seen well-laden outside the Belvoir Castle in Lower Bristol Road. (M.J. Tozer collection)*

*The flexibility of buses quickly made them popular for private hire work and FB02, a 32-seat Milnes Daimler, leads FB 07, a similar vehicle, through Burrington Combe. The precarious positions of some of the travellers is very apparent! (Jack Bishop collection)*

*Milnes Daimler FB 04 looks slightly top heavy when operating a private hire journey in this posed shot. It is thought that the photograph was taken in Frome on 30th May 1907. (Jack Bishop collection)*

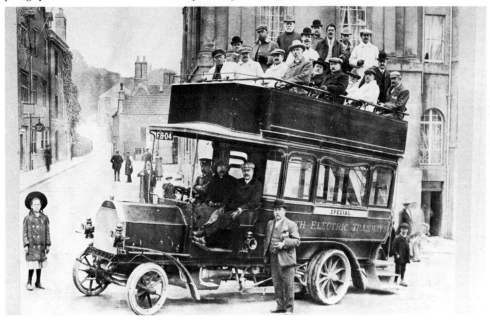

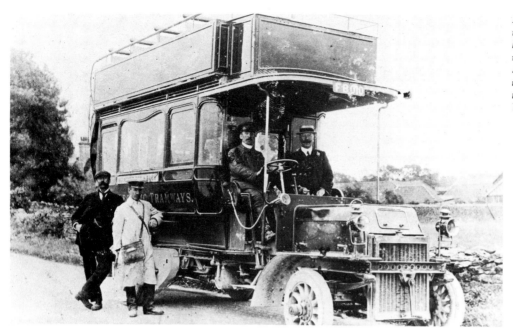

It is understood that the figure 0 was inserted between the registration letters and figures on Bath vehicles which were larger than motor cars. Straker Squires FB 010 displays this unusual feature when operating on the Melksham to Bath road. (Bristol Vintage Bus Group)

On Summer Sundays between 1919 and 1933 the Great Western Railway ran excursions from Paddington Station in London to Lavington Station near Devizes. There they were met by numerous coaches from the fleet of Lavington and Devizes Motor Services to take the passengers to a variety of tourist attractions including Stonehenge and Amesbury. Between 230 and 270 travellers were normally carried on the outings and later returned to Lavington Station for the return rail trip to London. Here a mixture of vehicles including AECs, Crossleys and Reos are lined up in the Market Place at Market Lavington on such an occasion. The company was later taken over by Bath Tramways. (Stan Weston)

*FB 027 was an AEC charabanc which was convertible to suit weather conditions. It is pictured with the canvas roof rolled back on a private hire trip. (Bristol Vintage Bus Group)*

people interested enough to invest in the project. Because of this, Bath Tramways Motor Company Ltd was formed on 30th July 1920 to take over the motorbuses and the foundry at the Walcot Street tram depot, which had been a lucrative part of the business, particularly during the war.

Bristol Tramways had been looking to expand and increase its operating area and on 2nd July 1909 introduced nine motor taxi cabs in Bath which quickly became known as 'The Blue Cabs'. Because of the popularity of the rival Bath trams and buses, however, the taxis were withdrawn by July 1921. In 1910 Bristol

Tramways introduced a charabanc tour from Bristol to the Bath Racecourse at Lansdown which was not served by any tram service but it was 1911 before the Bristol company was able to operate a charabanc into Bath due to strong objections from Bath Electric Tramways. Ultimately a garage to house the buses and charabancs based in Bath was opened in James Street West on a site now occupied by the Kingsmead Motor Company. Until the late 1960s the staff based at Bath and allocated to the Bristol routes were employed by the Bristol company rather than the Bath companies with consequent minor differences in conditions of employment.

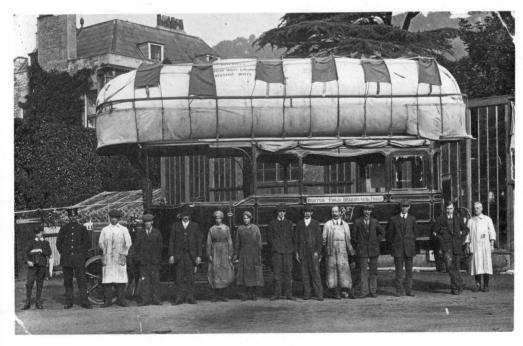

*During the First World War experiments were carried out with gas propulsion. The gas bag took up the whole of the top deck as can be seen in this view taken in Kensington Depot. (A. Merritt collection)*

The introduction of the Road Traffic Act of 1930 revolutionised the passenger transport industry. Before the Act there had not been any real control over bus routes and their operation but the Act formed Area Traffic Commissioners who had the power to grant or refuse any applications to operate bus services. Bus drivers and conductors were also now required by law to be licensed to carry out these duties and display a PSV badge indicating that this licence had been granted. This system replaced the previous arrangements where the local police or authority had enforced this task. Under the 1930 Act the Bath and Bristol companies came under the Western Area Traffic Commissioners whose offices were and still are based in Bristol.

*FB 5890 was a Bristol A complete with Bristol 36-seat bodywork. It was new in April 1927 and withdrawn from service in April 1939 when it was sold to AEC Engine Division in Southall for staff transport. (M.J. Tozer collection)*

When Bristol Tramways took over the two Bath companies in 1936 the Bath Tramways Motor Company owned over 90 vehicles of extremely varied ages and origins, although most were AECs, ADCs or Commers. In mid-1937 the average age of the fleet was improved when 20 new AECs with 35-seat Eastern Coachwork bodies were delivered, followed during the next 4 years by 3 AECs with Weymann 32-seat coach bodies and 24 Bristols with 32-seat bus bodywork. All buses originally purchased for the Bath companies were registered with FB or GL Bath registration marks. The new company was keen to replace trams with motorbuses and had already started to do this in Weston-super-Mare in April 1937 and Bristol in early May 1938. It was not surprising when announcements were made that the Bath trams were to be similarly treated between October 1938 and May 1939. They were replaced by Bristol K5G buses with 56-seat double-deck rear entrance bodies. In addition to these vehicles, 16 Bristol GO5G buses which had been equipped with Bristol 56-seat double-deck bodywork were purchased from Maidstone and District Motor Services Ltd and Chatham and District Traction Company in early 1939. These buses dated from 1936 and 1937 and were registered DKN 31 - DKN 46, and were bought without their original bodies. They were rebodied with new 56-seat double-deck bodies in Bristol or at Eastern Coachworks factory at Lowestoft. When those which had been dealt with at ECW arrived at Bath it was noted that they had DNK registrations instead of the correct DKN markings. Needless to say, this error was rectified before the buses entered service at Bath!

# TWENTY TIMES A DAY

# UP LANSDOWN HILL

(a two mile rise, including gradient of 1-7¼)

*Bath Tramways bought many AEC vehicles and the above advertisement appeared in the motor trade press. FB 8655 featured was new in August 1930 and carried Hall Lewis 32-seat front entrance bodywork. (M.J. Tozer collection)*

## AEC 'REGAL'

The Bath Tramways Motor Co. Ltd., which has standardised on  chassis since 1919, has placed in service a new fleet of six 'REGAL' Single Deckers. Practically all of this Company's routes, which extend for 20 miles around Bath, involve much stiff hill climbing.

Write for full particulars of the 'REGAL' 95 h.p. 6 cyl. 32 Seater Single Decker and other new Passenger Vehicles up to 68 Seaters

It was soon after the abandonment of the trams that the first effects of the Second World War were felt. Fuel rationing was introduced on 23rd September 1939 and resulted in a drastic reduction in levels of services, particularly during off-peak times, evenings and Sundays. At the end of September 1939 express services to the south west were withdrawn and by October 1942 all express operations had been suspended.

The war and blackout restrictions inevitably brought serious operating and staffing problems and led to the re-introduction of women for conducting duties. They were called conductresses or, sometimes, clippies, and their employment assisted in maintaining scheduled services. Due to restraints imposed by the Government on manufacturing industries, new buses became increasingly difficult to obtain and this resulted in secondhand vehicles being purchased or borrowed from other operators. Vehicles loaned to Bath Electric Tramways during the war included 2 open-staircase AEC Regents, dating from October 1931, registered GP 6239 and GP 6243. These were owned by Brighton Hove and District Omnibus Company Ltd and carried Tilling bodywork, seating 27 passengers on the upper deck and 25 in the lower saloon. These arrived in Bath in 1941 after they had spent a short time on Bristol city services and were

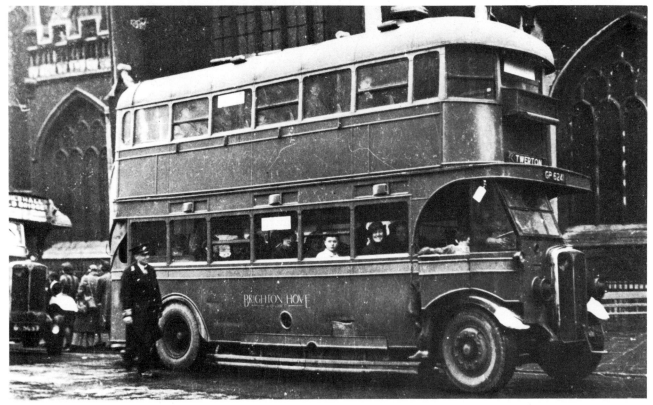

GP 6241 was number 6241 in the Brighton Hove and District fleet and is seen outside Bath Abbey when operating the Twerton service. It was not officially on loan to the Bath companies but to the Bristol concern. Note the headlamp masks and the white painted edges to the front mudguards. (S.L. Poole, courtesy London Bus Preservation Group)

returned to Brighton during the latter part of 1942. Five Leyland Tigress vehicles with Harrington 26-seat coach bodies, dating from May and June 1936, were loaned to Bristol Tramways by Devon General Omnibus and Touring Company Ltd from 1941 to 1943. These were registered AOD 599-603 and passed to Bath Tramways Motor Company in 1943.

In March 1943 a Leyland TS1 with Leyland 32-seat coach bodywork, which was new in February 1929, was loaned to Bath Tramways Motor Company. It was owned by H. Russett of Bristol, who traded as Royal Blue Coaches, and had originally been bought new by J. Watkinson of Preston who operated under the fleetname of Scout. This coach was purchased by Russett in November 1931 and was taken over by the Ministry of Transport in September 1939 for use by the War Department. It was eventually returned to Russett by the War Department in March 1942.

Between 1942 and 1946 the London Passenger Transport Board loaned 12 AEC Regents to the Bath and Bristol companies. They were fitted with 48-seat rear-entrance double-deck bodies manufactured by the London General Omnibus Company. Six of these vehicles were received by the Bath companies and were registered GH 582, GH 585, GK 3014, GK 3067, GK 3148 and GK 5305 and had carried fleet numbers

*Vehicles loaned to Bath Tramways included 12 AEC Regents with 48-seat bodies. They were eventually numbered into the fleet and ST 499 became 3833 (GK 3148), on loan from 1942 until 1946. It is seen outside Bath Abbey operating to Ascension Church. (W.J. Haynes)*

ST268/92, ST348/77 and ST499/95. From January 1944 they were numbered into the Bath fleets as 3830-3832, 3834, 3833 and 3835 respectively.

Many War Department establishments were set up in West Wiltshire and sites were particularly dense around the Corsham area, resulting in many forces personnel moving into the region to operate and control the sites. The initial building of these bases required a number of civilian workers and once completed, the sites needed a number of civilians to assist the forces personnel in ensuring the smooth running of the establishments. The Bath companies were very involved in transporting the staffs employed from Bath and the surrounding areas to the Corsham sites, an operation which continues today by Badgerline Limited – albeit on a very much smaller scale. The operation of these contracts resulted in a marked increase in the number of vehicles required and led to the acquisition and reappearance of Bristol B type buses, which have been described as prehistoric, and also the transfer of the open-staircase double-deckers to meet this demand.

*3807 (GL 6606) a Bristol K5G with Bristol 56-seat body was new in 1939 and purchased to replace the city's trams. It is seen at Kensington Depot in pristine condition after its body had been reconstructed by the Company in 1946. It was transferred to Gloucester City Services in November 1951, renumbered 1533, withdrawn in 1952 and sold to a scrap dealer in February 1953. (Bristol Vintage Bus Group)*

Despite the influx of these extra vehicles it was still difficult to cater for all passengers who wished to travel, and certain single-deck buses were converted to perimeter seating so that the central area of the bus was available for a substantial number of standing passengers. When such buses were converted they were allocated a V prefix to the fleet number, the V standing for Victory, and were legally permitted to carry 60 passengers in total. Eleven gas-producer trailers were used on buses based at Bath in an attempt to reduce the Company's reliance upon other fuels, which were already rationed.

When it was apparent that the Second World War was imminent, 3 single-deck buses were converted into ambulances at Bath and a further 13 were requisitioned from the Bath fleets during 1940 and 1941 thus worsening an already difficult vehicle position. The supply of new vehicles to the Bristol and Bath companies to replace time-expired and war-damaged stock was seriously short of the ideal number required. Only 42 vehicles, of which 24 were single-deckers, were received by the Bristol Company in 1942 for allocation to its Bristol, Bath, Gloucester and Weston-super-Mare areas. In 1943 this number had reduced to 35 vehicles which included 31 single-deckers and in 1944 the unbelievable total of two double-deck buses were received in the shape of Bristol K6As with Strachan 55-seat bodies.

*2260 (GL 7809) shows the single-door Bristol body. During the Second World War perimeter seating was installed and the bus renumbered V2260 between June 1942 and late 1945 after which it reverted to normal seating arrangements for 32 passengers. It was new in 1941 and withdrawn in June 1955 for scrap. (R.W. Gingell)*

The only major casualty to Bath Tramways property recorded during the hostilities was to the Bath depot safe which was buried without trace during an air raid. It was not until about ten years later during building work that the safe was recovered. The bank notes were found to be charred and in pieces but despite this they were sent away by the bank, identified as far as possible and a refund made to the Company. As vehicles were an extremely valuable asset during the war, many buses were parked around the city, including Victoria Park, to avoid any substantial losses should Kensington Depot be the target of a bombing raid.

It is interesting to note that during the time that both trams and buses were operated (before approximately 1914) trams were subject to separate legislation from buses, which led to some unusual occurrences in some cities, particularly in the early days. Motorbuses were originally restricted to a speed limit of 12 mph but trams were permitted to operate at 14 mph in many places and in Bath on the section of route between Newton St. Loe and Turnpike. There were reported incidents where a bus driver was charged by the police for driving in excess of 12 mph but a tram driver operating at 14 mph on the same road was exempt from prosecution!

*2237 (GL 6027) was a Bristol L5G with Bristol 32-seat two-door body. It was new in 1938, had its body reconstructed by Heaver in 1948, and was withdrawn and sold to a Cardiff dealer in November 1953. (R.F. Mack)*

*Sixteen Bristol GO5G buses were purchased to replace the Bath trams in 1939 and were received in chassis form. 3822 (DKN 39) was originally number 278 in the Maidstone and District fleet. It is seen carrying its third body, this time by Eastern Coachworks with seats for 56 passengers. New in December 1936, it was withdrawn in 1956. (M.J. Tozer)*

*3800 (GL6601), a Bristol K5G with Bristol 56-seat body, is operating Service 3 between Bathford and Combe Down and is seen climbing Wells Road in wartime conditions. The Bath fleetname shows up well. (S.L. Poole, courtesy London Bus Preservation Group)*

*3814 (DKN 31) was bought from Maidstone and District as a chassis only. It was rebodied with a Bristol 56-seat body to replace the Twerton trams. It is seen carrying its third body, this time by Eastern Coachworks with 59 seats, in the post war livery. (Bristol Vintage Bus Group)*

Following the return of peace after the war the Company was keen to update its fleet efficiently and effectively and to achieve this aim many chassis were rebodied by the Company itself or through Eastern Coachworks which was becoming well known as simply ECW. It was quite common for the body from one bus to be removed and transferred to the chassis of another bus whose body was being scrapped.

Male members of staff who were returning to the Company as drivers and conductors from the forces were each sent a letter by the manager indicating the Company's pleasure at their return. The contents of the letter were standard for all the men and read as follows:

JLP/OKS                              7th May 1946

Dear Smith,

It gives me pleasure on behalf of the Company and Management to extend to you a hearty welcome back to civilian life and duty.

In your absence and in consequence of the heavy call upon the Company's manpower during the War, the introduction of women and temporary directed men was inevitable.

Although generally speaking these have done a good job of work under very trying circumstances, the well disciplined pre-war male staff has been greatly missed and service to the public badly deteriorated.

I am sure that you will wish to bring about the speedy recovery of the good name and standard of efficiency which the bus service held in Bath in pre-war days, and I know that you will do your best by your good example to assist in bringing this about.

Yours faithfully,

J.L. Palmer
Manager

I wonder what type of response there would be if this style of letter was sent out by any manager of an industry employing both sexes today?

The first new buses for the Bath companies were two double-deckers which were delivered in 1947 for the Bath Tramways Motor Company. One was a Bristol K6B and the other a Bristol K5G, both of which were bodied by Eastern Coachworks with 55-seat rear entrance bodies. Later in the year, other new buses delivered to Bristol in 1947 were transferred to Bath

*3865 (LHU 988) was originally 3765 in the Bristol fleet. New in 1949, it is a Bristol K6B with ECW 59-seat body and is seen at the bottom of Wells Road on Service 4 to Midford Road from Larkhall in 1952. Note the painted out destination box over the rear platform and the roll of the body as it corners with a full passenger load. (P.R. Forsey)*

*Is 2271 (LHT 915), a Bristol L6B with ECW 35-seat rear-entrance bodywork, carrying an oversize destination blind or has the aperture shrunk? The destination indicator had been reduced upon repainting and was seen operating Service 6 to Glasshouse on 19th April 1956 at Parade Gardens. It was new in October 1948, transferred to Bristol Country Services in October 1959 and withdrawn in 1960. (P.R. Forsey)*

*Showing the full use of the destination box, 2285 (LHW 908) awaits departure time from Swainswick for Penn Lea Road on 18th March 1956. It is a Bristol L6B with ECW 35-seat rear-entrance body. New in 1949, it was withdrawn and sold in March 1963. (P.R. Forsey)*

8072 carried the Bristol coat of arms when it was C8072. It was transferred to Bath Tramways Motor Co in May 1967 and it is seen in the depot yard at Kensington carrying Bath Services fleet-names. New in July 1952, it was withdrawn in 1968 and sold to Brains Foods of Short-wood near Bristol in April 1968 and from there was sold to a dealer in November 1981. It was purchased for preservation in November 1983. Un-like buses new to Bath, this one was equipped with a route number box only at the rear. (Bristol Vintage Bus Group)

and usually renumbered from their original fleet numbers. The separate fleet numbering systems used for Bath, Bristol and Gloucester led to much confusion at times, irrespective of where the vehicle was being transferred to or from!

Under the 1947 Transport Act, which saw a major post-war reorganisation of bus companies, the Bristol and Bath companies were sold to the British Transport Commission along with all other bus companies which were owned by the Transport Holding Co., part of the Thomas Tilling Group.

*Four Bristol SUS4A 30-seaters were received by Bristol Omnibus in September 1963. Numbers 303 and 304 were owned by Bath Tramways Motor Co. No 304 seen operating the Pump Room Special service normally run with the Trojan was withdrawn in 1969 and sold to Thames Valley Traction Co for further service and eventually scrapped in July 1972. (R.F. Mack)*

*An unusual acquisition in June 1963 was a Trojan 13-seat minibus. It was new to Silver Star Motor Services of Porton Down near Salisbury in February 1961 and passed to Wilts and Dorset when they bought Silver Star on 26th June 1963. The Trojan was numbered 2049 and painted in a special livery for a service between the Abbey, Roman Baths and the Assembly Rooms. It is seen in its first livery on 7th August 1963. It received a special livery in blue for this service in May 1967 and was withdrawn in 1970 after being renumbered to 400. (P.R. Forsey)*

This photograph clearly illustrates the unusual opening windows on the front upper deck of Bristol K6B 3842 (LHU 986). New in January 1949 to Bath Electric Tramways it was ...en transferred to Bath Tramways Motor Co in April 1950 and withdrawn from service in February 1966, after which it was sold for further use with L Margo of Southwest ...ndon. It was finally scrapped in February 1968. It is seen in healthier days behind Bath Bus Station on Service 19 on 12th July 1961. (P.R. Forsey)

*During its life 3647 (HHY 591) carried three different bodies. It was delivered in January 1945 with a Strachans 55-seat lowbridge body on its Bristol K6A chassis which was finished to Ministry of Supply regulations and the standard Tilling green livery of the day. An 'L' prefix was allocated in 1946 and in February 1954 it was fitted with a secondhand Duple body from bus L4146 which had been built in December 1941. The bus was renumbered 3789 in October 1955 when it received its third and final body, this time an ECW 59-seat highbridge body which was new in October 1949. It was eventually withdrawn from service in 1963 and sold for scrap in March 1964. It is seen in happier times at Grand Parade operating Service 46 to Calne carrying the Duple body and Bristol crest. (Bristol Vintage Bus Group)*

A revolutionary innovation in double-deck bus design occurred in October 1949 when the prototype Bristol Lodekka entered service in Bristol bearing fleet number C5000, later renumbered LC5000. The vehicle design allowed a highbridge style seating layout with a central upper-deck gangway to be used within the limitations of a lowbridge body. Before this, a lowbridge body needed an offside sunken gangway, with four abreast seating in the upper deck and an obtrusive offside projection into the lower saloon on which passengers were very prone to hit their heads. The seating and height allowance in the upper deck on these buses resulted in very cramped conditions and skittle alley buses, as they were known at Bath by the crews, were particularly unpopular with conductors and conductresses. One reason for their dislike of these vehicles was that to obtain fares from passengers sitting by the nearside windows upstairs, they needed either to lean across the other three passengers sitting nearer the gangway, or the other passengers had to pass across the coins and then receive the ticket and any change necessary.

The introduction of the Lodekka bus certainly assisted in the allocation of buses to routes at Bath. Many main roads in its operating area were obstructed by low bridges, invariably on trunk routes requiring the use of double-deck vehicles. Certain of these bridges have now been removed, the most noticeable being the one at Bathampton Dry Arch on the A36 from Bath to Warminster.

An unusual conversion for three Bath buses took place in 1952 and 1953 when three Bristol K5Gs, with Bristol 56-seat double-deck bodies, were converted to open top. In January 1952 buses 3811 and 3813 (GL 6612 and GL 6614) were rebuilt to permanent open-top and repainted in a reversed livery of mainly cream with green lining. They were renumbered 3614 and 3615 and transferred to Bristol Country Services for the sea-front service at Weston-super-Mare. In May 1953 similar bus 3810 (GL 6611) was also converted to open-top, renumbered 3616 and transferred to Weston to join the other 2 K5Gs on the promenade service. All 3 buses continued to give sterling service on the sea-front at Weston until the arrival of 4 new purpose-built, convertible, open-top Bristol FS6G buses which were delivered in November 1961. Both 3614 and 3616 were sold in November 1961 to the Southern Vectis Omnibus Company Ltd for continued use as open toppers on the Isle of Wight, but 3616 was sold to a dealer in April 1963 and scrapped in December 1963, 3614 following a similar fate in August 1965. Vehicle 3615, however, had a shorter life and was scrapped by a Leeds dealer in October 1961 immediately following withdrawal from revenue-earning service at Weston-super-Mare.

The familiar layout of double-deck buses remained unchanged, with a rear entrance, sometimes with platform doors, and an engine beside the driver at the front until 1959 when a front entrance Bristol Lodekka was designed and built. From 1960, numerous front entrance Lodekkas of 30 feet in length, seating 70 passengers (known as the FLF) or 27 feet 6 inches in length with seating for 60 passengers (FSF), were delivered together with the standard rear entrance Lodekkas (known as the LD or FS). Fluorescent lighting in both the upper and lower saloons on these buses improved conditions for both the passengers and staff, and air suspension on the rear axle improved comfort and riding qualities. On some FSF and FLF vehicles, exterior illuminated panels were fitted on the offside, and it was hoped that extra revenue from advertisers would be generated by this feature. This hope did not materialise and after 1963 no buses delivered to Bristol Omnibus Company, the revised company title from 1957, were equipped with exterior illuminated advertisement panels.

*L8133 (PHW 958) was one of six prototype Lodekkas and was delivered in March 1953 complete with an ECW 58-seat body. It was loaned to Red and White Services Ltd of Chepstow during May and June 1953. It was transferred to Bath Tramways Motor Co in June 1956 and withdrawn from service in 1968 after losing its distinctive radiator grille in January of that year. It was kept by Bristol Omnibus from February 1968 until May 1977 as a possible preservation candidate but was, unfortunately, sold for scrap in May 1977. (R.F. Mack)*

The traditional single-deck vehicle layout, with an engine at the front beside the driver and a front or rear entrance, remained unchanged until 1951 when, in January, an underfloor-engined Bristol LS with bodywork by ECW was delivered to Bristol Tramways. It featured both a front and rear doorway and had a seating capacity of 42 passengers. It was painted in a different livery to the standard, with green below the waistrail and cream above. It was easily identified because it was equipped with a Tilling 3-piece destination box at the front and a 2-piece side by side display at the rear. This bus was loaned to Bath Tramways Motor Company and used on various services during November and December 1952. The vehicle was later modified to front entrance only, equipped with a Gardner 5HLW engine instead of the original Bristol XWA, and fitted with 8-feet wide axles. It returned to service as a 44-seater with Bristol by February 1956, carrying the standard green livery and single blind destination displays.

*8018 (NAE 50) is a KS6B with ECW 60-seat body and was received in March 1951. The overhang of the body beyond the wheels is due to the body being 8 feet wide and the chassis only 7 feet 6 inches. Originally owned by Bath Tramways Motor Co it was transferred to Bath Electric Tramways in January 1958. It was initially fitted with a one-piece destination box which was later replaced by the T type indicator shown. It was withdrawn in 1968 and sold for scrap. The uninformative display SERVICE does not reveal that it is operating between Elmhurst Estate and Foxhill Estate. (Bristol Vintage Bus Group)*

*Proudly proclaiming that its body was made by Eastern Coachworks, L8536 (988 EHW) is caught by the camera on delivery to Bath Tramways Motor Co in October 1959. The radiators either side of the destination box were for the Cave-Brown-Cave heating system. In August 1967 this bus was transferred to Bath Electric Tramways and in January 1976 converted into Driver Tuition Vehicle No W156 until it was withdrawn and scrapped in June 1981. (Bristol Vintage Bus Group)*

On 7th June 1960, when 8266 (UHY 377) was captured at Bath Bus Station, buses reversed onto the stands. With the increase in front entrance buses, arrangements were later altered so that buses reversed from the stands. Note the platform doors, by then considered desirable for country routes. Service 64 operated from Bath to Frome "round the houses" as was known to the crews. (P.R. Forsey)

*2828 (PHW 918) was finished in Green Line livery for extensive trials with London Transport after initial work with Bath Tramways. Seen at Old Bridge, Bath on 26th February 1953, it shows the three piece Tilling type destination display. The inspector is Jim Vaughan, the author's late father-in-law. (P.R. Forsey)*

Another LS vehicle which attracted attention when it was allocated to Bath Tramways Motor Company during February and March 1953 was vehicle 2828 (PHW 918). It was operated in the full Lincoln green Green Line livery of London Transport, with 3-piece destination displays at the front and rear. In April 1953 this bus entered service with London Transport on route 447 at Reigate garage until July 1953 when it was allocated to route 711. In August 1953 the bus was fitted with a Hobbs semi-automatic gearbox and reallocated to route 447. During November 1953, 2828 was sent to Dalston garage for use on London Transport routes 208 and 208A but returned to Reigate and route 447 in March 1954. The Hobbs transmission was removed from the vehicle in April 1954 and the bus was returned to Bristol Tramways.

The Tilling destination displays were replaced with standard single aperture destination boxes at the front and rear and the vehicle received standard Bristol livery in May 1954, eventually being modified for one man operation in January 1957. From the mid-1950s the Company was giving serious consideration to one man operation of certain services and from 1957 infrequent routes such as that between Bath and Upper Westwood were converted to o.m.o. to reduce the requirement for conductors and in turn reduce operating costs.

The city routes in Bath were and continue to be run from bus stops on the streets and until Bath Bus Station was opened in March 1958 three different street sites were used to operate the country services. Routes operating principally on the northern side of the River Avon to places such as Chippenham,

*3001 (XHW 420) was originally 2904 in 1957. The Company experimented with upgrading buses by refurbishing much of the bodywork in 1971. It was found that the cost of this work was too expensive and only a few vehicles were similarly treated. It was withdrawn for scrap in 1977. (A.R. Macfarlane)*

Trowbridge and Marshfield departed from stops on Grand Parade. Those routes operating southwards from Bath to places such as Wells, Shepton Mallet and the Midsomer Norton/Radstock areas ran from the south side of Old Bridge, which was later demolished and replaced by Churchill Bridge, on a site slightly downstream, in 1966. To complicate matters even further, the buses to Bristol via Keynsham or via Kelston and Bitton, departed from bus stops at Queen's Parade on the north side of Queen Square. Any country passenger wishing to travel to Bath and change to another country service quite often had an arduous walk to face once they had reached Bath, particularly if they had arrived from Trowbridge or Chippenham and wished to continue to Bristol.

On a wet day in July 1957, 2913 (YHY 71), a Bristol LS5G with ECW 45-seat front entrance body, is operating on Service 10 to Swainswick. Delivered in August 1957, this bus remained at Bath until withdrawal for scrap in August 1972. (P.R. Forsey)

Supervision of the 3 departure sites by an Inspector was a cost which was significantly reduced by the opening of Bath Bus Station, when all country services were transferred from the streets. All ticket machines, the cash office and associated equipment for cash counting were removed from Kensington Depot to the Bus Station and the previous situation, where buses had operated on service when running in from the City Centre to the Depot, ceased because conductors, in the main, both reported and booked off at the Bus Station.

*Kensington Depot was completely upgraded during 1961 and 1962 and at times a number of buses were parked overnight at the Bus Station. A variety of buses form the background to this scene. (Stothert & Pitt Ltd, courtesy F.E. Dark)*

Improvements and upgrading of engineering facilities at Kensington Depot took place in 1961 and 1962 and the corrugated sheds were replaced by an open yard, with a mechanical bus wash, for storage of the buses and a modern purpose-built workshop and administration block for the maintenance of the fleet.

During the 1960s and 1970s it was extremely difficult to recruit sufficient drivers and conductors to maintain the advertised service levels and reliability of routes was badly affected. In 1967 a new style of single-deck bus, purpose-built for one man operation, was introduced on certain city routes. The vehicle was known as the Bristol RELL and had a seating capacity of 53 passengers. The intention ultimately was to operate these vehicles as one man buses although they were initially used with conductors. It was hoped that reliability on routes would be improved as they needed

only a driver and not a crew of two. Until the early 1960s it was only legal to operate a single-deck bus without a conductor and it was not until the 1970s that the Company considered one man operation of services with double-deck vehicles to be an alternative to single-deck o.m.o. in places outside Bristol.

The 1968 Transport Act of the Labour government resulted in the formation of the National Bus Company on 1st January 1969. NBC was formed by the combination of companies controlled by British Electric Traction (BET) and the Transport Holding Company (THC). THC had been known as the Tilling Group until 1948 and between 1948 and 1962 as the British Transport Commission. The Bath and Bristol companies which were controlled by THC were, therefore, transferred to NBC.

*Marshfield is the setting for Bristol MW5G 2975 (987 EHY) returning to its home at Bath. Received in October 1959, it survived until January 1976 when it was sold to a dealer in Yorkshire who later resold it to a Doncaster scout group, who themselves sold it again to a dealer in 1981. (R.F. Mack)*

*Conversion of services to one man operation resulted in the introduction of the Bristol RELL6L with ECW 53-seat bodies, some of which were later altered to two-door. 1021 (MAE 24F) was delivered in August 1967 and was selected for a revised fleetname showing the city crest and advertisement arrangement for two-door models, hence the well set-back Bristol Greyhound poster. Withdrawn in May 1982 it was later scrapped. It is seen here on Service 201 to Larkhall in December 1967. (Bristol Vintage Bus Group)*

*Originally 3768 (LHU 990), this Bristol K6B with ECW 59-seat body was renumbered 3868 when it was sent to Bath Electric Tramways during September 1949. Delivered June 1949, it survived until it was withdrawn for scrap in September 1966. (P.R. Forsey)*

By the time that this photograph was taken on 27th March 1961, the Old Bridge was showing signs of weakness after flood damage. Bristol K6A 3831 (JHT 112) is seen crossing the bridge during reinforcing work. The bus was new in 1946 and carried a Duple 56-seat body to Ministry of Supply specifications. This was replaced in February 1956 by an ECW 56-seat body which was new in February 1949 from bus 3820. It was withdrawn for scrap in July 1964. (P.R. Forsey)

*During its life at Bath L8243 (THW 733) received a shorter radiator grille and hopper type ventilators in the front upper-deck windows. It is seen at the bottom of Milso Street on Service 2 to Combe Down Church on 21st May 1962. New in March 1955, it retained Bath Services fleetnames until it was withdrawn for scrap in August 1970. (P. Forsey)*

L8450 (YHT 962) was a Bristol LDL6G with 30 foot long, 70-seat ECW body with rear entrance and platform doors. It was transferred to Bath Tramways Motor Co in December 1963 and was one of only six LDLs built in 1957. It was often to be seen operating between Bath and Colerne on Service 51, later renumbered to 230 in 1967. The extra length can be identified by the additional small window towards the rear of the bus. It was withdrawn and sold to a dealer in January 1976. (R.F. Mack/Bristol Vintage Bus Group)

An inspector stands on the platform edge of Bristol K6B 3872 (LHU 994) as it operates on Service 4 to Larkhall outside the Guildhall on 2nd October 1954. Originally numbered 3772 when new in June 1949, it was renumbered when transferred to Bath Tramways Motor Co in September 1949. Note the panelled-over side destination box over the platform, the short-lived livery and destination display. This bus was withdrawn and scrapped in 1966. (Peter G. Davey)

*Received in October 1956, L8384 (WHY 939) carried an ECW 58-seat open platform rear-entrance body. Classified as a Bristol LD6B, it retained Bath Services fleetnames until Bristol fleetnames were substituted in 1972. It was withdrawn in August 1972 and sold for scrap. Inspector Jim Vaughan, the author's late father-in-law, is riding as passenger on the upper deck on 26th October 1971. (A.R. Macfarlane)*

On 1st January 1970 both Bath Electric Tramways Ltd and Bath Tramways Motor Company Ltd were wound up and officially transferred to Bristol Omnibus Company Ltd. Before this, separate accounts and vehicles were kept for each of the Bath companies and, in theory at least, if a BET bus was used on a BTM route, or vice versa, such usage was noted so that appropriate mileage and costs could be claimed from the other company.

On Saturday 18th October 1980 the last double-deck crew-operated buses ran on Services 203 and 213 between Foxhill Estate and Bathford or Elmhurst Estate and between Bath and Bristol via Keynsham on Service 339. The following day all services from Bath depot were converted to one man operation which resulted in the remaining conductors, conductresses and drivers, who did not wish to transfer to o.m.o. duties, being made redundant.

*Devizes Depot in Station Road is the setting for L8496 (856 CHU) a Bristol LD6G with ECW 58-seat rear-entrance bodywork with platform doors. Note the metal advertisements on the wall. The bus is due to operate on Service 50A although the 5 and A are a little difficult to read. Received in February 1959 by Bath Electric Tramways, it was withdrawn from service in May 1975 and scrapped. (R.F. Mack)*

The Bristol FLF was taken into the fleet with either Bristol or Gardner engines and one example at Bath was equipped with a Leyland unit. 7249 (FHU 507D) is a Bristol-engined version and is pictured at the old Elmhurst terminus at Catherine Way on 11th March 1978. New in February 1966 it was sold in December 1982. (D.G. Ormiston)

On 11th September 1983 the Bristol Omnibus Company was divided so that the northern area covering Gloucester, Cheltenham, Swindon and Stroud was transferred to a new company called the Cheltenham and Gloucester Omnibus Company Ltd. The remaining part of the company was also divided into Bristol City Bus, which controlled the city services in Bristol itself, and Bristol Country Bus, which included the services in and around Bath and Weston-super-Mare and the country services operating from Bristol Bus Station. A new fleetname, Badgerline, with a striking livery was launched on 29th April 1985 as a marketing identity for all services which had been transferred to Bristol Country Bus. On 1st January 1986 the unit became a legally separate company called Badgerline Ltd and the head office of the new company has now been transferred from Berkeley House at Lawrence Hill in Bristol to Badger House at Oldmixon Crescent in Weston-super-Mare.

The Badgerline livery for standard service buses includes a yellow front well displayed by RELL6L 1304 (HHW 917L). New in 1972, it is still in service with the Company although de-licensed. The rear of Ford Transit minibus 4511 (C511 BFB) can also be seen. (Stephen White)

*The Bristol VRT has been the standard one person double-deck bus for some years although they are no longer built and have been replaced by the Leyland Olympian. An early series 3 Gardner engined VRT, 5505 (KOU 791P) is operating Service 13A from Elmhurst Estate to Ralph Allen School on 3rd October 1984. Note the BATH fleetname. It was new in 1976. (A.R. Macfarlane)*

*Five MCW Metrobuses with Rolls Royce power units were delivered in 1980 and initially used on Services 203 and 213, later renumbered 3 and 13. They were selected for fitting of coach seats and were then reallocated to the Bristol services. On 9th January 1982, 6000 (DAE 510W) is stranded in snow at Brislington as were many buses both in and outside the Bath area. (M.S. Curtis)*

*Bath had not received any of the W registration Bristol VRTs when new. Six are now allocated to the depot including two equipped with Transign destination boxes. Automatic gearboxes are fitted but not liked by all drivers although the Leyland 0680 engines give plenty of power with a distinctive roar to the exhaust. 5531 (EWS 739W) was new in 1981 and transferred to Bath on 22nd September 1984. All six are usually to be found on Services 3, 13 and 23, and 5531 was at Elmhurst Estate on 29th September 1984 still carrying Weston and Wells fleetnames and WM depot allocation plates instead of BH. Note the BATH local identity bus stop flag. (S.M. Chislett)*

# CHAPTER 4 – COACHES WITHOUT HORSES

Bath, the jewel of the West Country, has always been a major attraction to visitors from all over the world and coaches on express services and private hire or tour work have frequently catered for this demand. The Bath Tramways Motor Company owned a fleet of charabancs from 1905 which were quickly advertised, perhaps unfortunately, as "The Green Torpedo Cars"! The original Torpedo House booking office was in Upper Borough Walls but later moved to 10 Northgate Street, where the Company's main offices remained until the Bus Station complex was completed in March 1958.

Early advertisements describing the charabancs as giving reliability, comfort, elegance and speed, stated that they were freely available for private hire. Later when 28-seater "super all-weather" vehicles arrived, the description was amended to explain that these were luxuriously upholstered and well-sprung, in fact the very acme of comfort.

Bath Tramways proclaimed in its publicity that they were the pioneers of Motor Touring in the "West Countrie". Tours run by the Company originally started from outside the Guildhall but later moved to Torpedo House in Northgate Street before proceeding to Grand Parade to pick up any further passengers. Since the earliest days, conducted tours of the city and the popular destinations of Cheddar, Wookey Hole, Wells, Longleat and other local places of interest have been included in the extensive list of tours. These have been run to the present day except for a relatively short period in the late 1970s when coaching activities were abandoned for a few years.

The early tour booklets detailed the major points of interest to be seen during the tour and were printed on glossy paper amounting to at least 80 pages with stapled card covers. An interesting advertisement contained in the booklet was for the Glasshouse Cafe and Tea Gardens, owned by Bath Electric Tramways, which advised the public that for an enjoyable afternoon they should take the tram from the Guildhall and book to the Glasshouse Cafe. It added: 'You will be agreeably surprised'. Private parties hiring vehicles were encouraged, whenever possible, to use these facilities as a refreshment stop and certain tours were scheduled to call at the Cafe for tea or a refreshment break.

One booklet lists no less than 9 afternoon tours all leaving Grand Parade at 15.15 every day, including Sundays, for a price of 2/6 (12½p) per head including tea. It concludes by saying that this was the 'finest value Bath has to offer its Visitor'. The afternoon circular tours varied in journey length from 18 to 24 miles. A summary of the tours offered was Tour No. 1 – Farleigh Wick, Bradford-on-Avon and Monkton Combe Village; No 2 – Kelston, Bitton and Keynsham; No. 3 – Wick and Lansdown; No. 4 – Wolverton,

*Postcards of trams and buses were extremely popular until the 1920s and Bath's Green Torpedoes running tours were no exception as this postcard proves. The charabanc is seen fully loaded outside the Guildhall. (Jack Bishop collection – Celesque Series postcard)*

A Souvenir of a Tour by a Green Torpedo Motor Car from Bath to Cheddar, Glastonbury, and Wells.

Seen in Railway Street at the rear of Bath Bus Station, 2057 (NAE 8) was a Bristol LL6B with 35-seat coach style ECW body. It was delivered in March 1951 as 2805 but renumbered to 2057 in March 1961 when it also received the Bristol Greyhound livery shown. It was sold to a coach operator in August 1964 who withdrew it from service in December 1965. It was photographed on 13th June 1962. (A.R. Macfarlane)

New in June 1955 and originally allocated fleet number 2882 (THY 956), by the time this photograph was taken on 9th September 1965 this Bristol LS6G had been renumbered 2104. It carried an ECW 39-seat coach style body which was standard in many bus fleets in the '50s and '60s. Withdrawn in 1967, it saw further use with a London tour operator until it was scrapped in 1972. (A.R. Macfarlane)

Some people feel that the styling of 2154 (NHW 311F) was too bus-like, but the Bristol RELH6L gave a speedier and more comfortable ride than that given by earlier coaches. First licensed on 1st May 1968, it is seen on 23rd May 1968 leaving Bath Bus Station for London in Bristol Greyhound livery. It had coach seating for 45 passengers. (A.R. Macfarlane)

*2090 (EHW 314K) was employed on coaching work when new. It had been downgraded to dual purpose duties when this view was taken in the late 1970s. A shortage of FLF double-decks has led to Leyland Leopard 2090 being allocated to a crew working on Service 213. (D. Withers/BVBG)*

Norton St. Philip and Midford; No. 5 – Batheaston, Box Hill, Chapel Plaster, Kingsdown and Lambridge; No. 6 – Peasedown, Radstock, Writhlington, Faulkland, Norton St. Philip and Midford; No. 7 – Kelston, Bitton, Bridge Yate, Wick and Lansdown; No. 8 – Bathford, Kingsdown, Horse and Jockey, Bradford Leigh, Sally-in-the-Wood and Lambridge; and No. 9 – Zorston (presumably supposed to be Corston), Marksbury, Chelwood Bridge, North End, Kingwell Hall, Timsbury, Tunley and Odd Down. From this list it is obvious that a lengthy deviation was required on some of the tours to get from the finishing point to Glasshouse!

A regular private hire contract for the Company since the 1950s has been the transportation of French students in England attending Mons. Chassang's school in Paris. The number of students has required as many as 10 coaches to collect them on arrival in Southern England, bring them to Bath and return them to the South Coast after about a month's stay in Bath. Tours to places of interest selected by the organisers are always included in their itinerary and the Company has supplied vehicles or sub-contracted the work.

Tours to places outside Bath became extremely popular between the 1950s and the mid-1970s and this demand was met by Bath Tramways operating an extensive programme of full day, half-day and evening tours or excursions. The conducted City Tour was run twice daily, except Saturdays, with a guide who gave a comprehensive history on points of interest during the tour. Some of these City Tour guides are now Inspectors or Senior Inspectors at Bath and give conducted City Tours when the occasion demands. City Tours were suspended in the late 1970s when the coaches were withdrawn from the fleet, but with the recent upturn in the coaching market the Company reintroduced coach services substantially from 1983.

Express services, before the formation of the National Bus Company in 1969, were operated in agreement with the Associated Motorways, and services were run by the Bath companies under the Bristol Greyhound name. Other companies running services with Bristol Greyhound included Royal Blue of Exeter and Black and White Motorways of Cheltenham. The opening of many sections of motorway, particularly the M4, during the 1960s and 1970s enabled express services to be speeded up, making the use of coaches for long distance journeys, and in particular to London, much more attractive to passengers. The profitability of running coaches from Bath to London along the old A4 road through Chippenham, Marlborough, Newbury and Reading was affected by the new motorways and resulted in cuts in the number of journeys operating via the slower routes.

Today Badgerline continues to offer coach tours and private hire facilities and provides staff and vehicles for National Express Service 603 between Bath, Wells or Frome and London.

*2104 (WFH 169S) was purchased from National Travel (South West) in 1983. Built in 1978, it is a Leyland Leopard with Plaxton Supreme Express bodywork for 53 passengers. It is pictured at Bath Bus Station operating on National Express Service 603 between Bath and London. Note the Badgerline fleetname which had replaced the BATH local fleetname. (Stephen White)*

*An MCW Metroliner double-deck coach was borrowed from National Travel (West) during July 1984 for use on National Express Service 603 from Bath. Finished to Rapide specifications, it was equipped with video screens on both decks and a toilet and galley area on the lower deck. Seating was provided for 73 passengers of which 55 were on the top deck. It kept its NT number of 117 during its short stay at Bath (A117 KBA). It was caught at Green Park Road, Bath on 4th July 1984. (S.M. Chislett)*

*2209 (A209 SAE) displays its BATH local identity at Bath Bus Station before operating an afternoon tour to the ever popular destination of Cheddar and Wells. It is a Leyland Tiger with Plaxton Paramount 53-seat body and was new in 1983. (Stephen White)*

# CHAPTER 5 – TOPLESS IN BATH!

Open-top double-deck buses are usually associated with and have long been an accepted part of sea-front services in coastal towns such as Torquay, Paignton or even Weston-super-Mare. Although ways of generating additional revenue were continually being investigated, it was quite a surprise when open top buses were introduced onto a circular service at Bath on 29th May 1983.

The idea to run this service came from Mike Walker, the Area Traffic Superintendent for Bath, who had considerable experience of this type of service at Weston-super-Mare. The route was planned to cover some of the attractive parts of the city and to serve as many of the main places of interest as possible within the limited resources that would be available. It was decided to operate the service from the Bus Station via the Abbey, Assembly Rooms, Circus and Royal Crescent, catering primarily for tourists and replacing the conducted tours which had been run by the

Company but abandoned along with the other coaching activities in the late 1970s.

The service was licensed to run daily until 29th August and permanent open-top Leyland Atlantean No. 8600 (HOR 592E recently re-registered with cherished number VCL 461) was transferred from Weston-super-Mare to Bath to operate this service. Seven journeys a day were scheduled to run every hour from 10.05, except that on Sundays the timetable started at 13.05, and the route ran from the Bus Station, being scheduled to stop at Terrace Walk for the Fernley Hotel, Bath Abbey, Walcot Street for the Beaufort Hotel, Bennett Street for the Assembly Rooms, Royal Crescent, Milsom Street for the Royal Photographic Society, Terrace Walk again, the Bus Station, Prior Park College, Bath University, Norwood Avenue for the American Museum, Bathwick Hill for the Youth Hostel, Great Pulteney Street for the Holburne Museum, Terrace Walk and back again to the Bus Station with,

*3616 (GL 6611) was originally 3810 in the Bath Tramways fleet. New in May 1939, it was one of a batch of Bristol K5Gs purchased to replace the Bath trams. It was delivered with a Bristol 56-seat body and operated Bath area services until May 1953 when it was selected for conversion to open-top for use on the Sea Front service at Weston-Super-Mare. In November 1961 it was replaced by convertible open-top FS6Gs, sold to Southern Vectis and eventually scrapped in December 1963. (P.R. Forsey)*

hopefully, 5 minutes before the next departure! This resulted in a figure of eight service covering a sizeable portion of the city. Special fares were introduced and passengers could buy a Day Ticket which allowed unlimited use of the service on the day of issue. These tickets have also permitted the passenger reduced entry fees to certain museums and other attractions. Also available were Round Trip tickets, allowing one complete circuit of the route, and a Short Hop ticket for any journey wholly within the section of route between the Bus Station and Assembly Rooms. The Short Hop fare was not well used and was abandoned after a year.

*8600 (HOR 592E) was bought by R. Chisnell who operated services in the Winchester area under the King Alfred fleetname. It was built in 1967 and taken over by Hants and Dorset when the business was purchased in April 1973 and numbered 2304. In March 1979 it was purchased by Bristol Omnibus and converted to permanent open-top. It commenced service in October 1979 in all cream livery which was replaced by the white and blue Coastrider livery for the 1982 summer season at Weston. It was again repainted all white for the start of the open top service in Bath in 1983. It is seen near Bath Abbey on 19th August 1983 with an open-top VRT loaned from Devon General in exchange for a two-door Bristol City VRT. Service number 51 is allocated but not always displayed on the buses. (A.R. Macfarlane)*

*Proudly announcing that it belongs to Bath, 8607 (UFX 859S) is seen at Parade Gardens on 2nd September 1984, its first season at Bath following its transfer from Weston. The livery is cream and green. (M.S. Curtis)*

The Summer of 1983 brought plenty of hot weather and Bath basked in a tropical heatwave. The poor old Atlantean was unable to cope with the numbers of passengers wishing to travel and help arrived in the shape of a convertible open-top Bristol VRT from Devon General. Weston-super-Mare was not able to assist at this time as their open-toppers were all committed to the operation of sea-front services at Weston and Burnham-on-Sea. The red and white Devon General bus, exchanged for a two-door Bristol city VRT, was rapidly put into service and quickly earned its keep alongside the Atlantean. The borrowed bus, No. 935 (VDV 135S) in the Devon General fleet and named Triumph, was returned to its owners at the end of the particularly successful first open-top season at Bath.

To meet a demand for earlier journeys on Sundays, the Company applied to the Traffic Commissioners to run all journeys daily. This application was granted and started on Sunday 19th June 1983, so that the seven journeys ran throughout the week. Publicity for the new service announced that "Bath's new open-top bus will open up Bath to you!" and it certainly opened up a new revenue source for the Company.

For the 1984 season the timetable was increased from hourly to half-hourly intervals and the section of route via Saracen Street to Walcot Street for the Beaufort Hotel withdrawn due to lack of trade at that stop – although it would have been extremely difficult to accommodate any intending passengers anyway!

*Originally a two-door bus, permanent open-top VRT 8615 (JHW 107P) returns towards the Bus Station on 9th September 1985. It was C5033 in the Bristol City fleet but lost the C prefix in August 1978. It was transferred to Weston on 25th January 1981 following the MAP surveys which showed an increased requirement for double-decks at Weston and Bath. It was re-engined from a Leyland 501 unit to a Gardner 6LXB in September 1983 and converted to open-top by Hants and Dorset Engineering early in 1985. (A.R. Macfarlane)*

The improved service level was met by the transfer of convertible open top VRTs 8607 and 8608 from Weston-super-Mare which were released by the arrival of new convertible Roe-bodied Leyland Olympians. VRTs 8607 and 8608 had been purchased by Hants and Dorset in 1977 but, because of service revisions with Bournemouth Transport Department, the Hants and Dorset Company lost their open top services, although they had 6 suitable buses to operate them!

In 1979 Southern Vectis, the National Bus Company on the Isle of Wight, swapped 6 standard VRTs for these and in 1983 agreed to exchange 2 of these newly inherited convertibles for 2 fixed top Bristol VRTs, one of which was based at Bath. The Summer of 1984 again resulted in a high demand for the open-top service in the city and arrangements were made to obtain a further suitable vehicle to alleviate the overloading problems. Agreement was reached with Southdown Motor Services to swap a standard VRT from Bath for a convertible VRT at Hilsea and Bath bus 5522 (PEU 517R) was exchanged with Southdown 605 (UWV 605S) on 26th June for the remainder of the season. The roof had been removed from vehicle 605 before it was collected by the staff at Southdown and the Bath VRT was a source of interest to Southdown drivers as it was fitted with a Webasto cab heater unlike

*The summer of 1984 proved to be almost as hot and sunny as the previous year and assistance was required to cope with the passenger loadings. Help arrived on 26th June when Southdown 605 (UWV 605 S) was swopped for a fixed-top VRT. It is seen here earning its keep at the Bus Station during July, showing 000 in the rear route-number box, although it did sometimes display 51. (S.M. Chislett)*

any of their vehicles. The Southdown bus was easily recognised as it was fitted with a rear route number indicator which frequently displayed 51 – the open-top service number.

The 1985 Summer season resulted in the open-top service offering a 20-minute frequency during April, May, September and October and a 15-minute frequency during June, July and August. This service was marketed under the Scenic Tour title and a fully conducted tour lasting approximately 1½ hours was operated 4 times a day betwen May and August under the Heritage Tour title using Leyland Atlantean 8600.

In 1984 a tannoy system was in operation on the Scenic Tour over which the driver pointed out items of interest during the journey. This practice continues although, in an attempt to overcome objections from the residents in some sensitive parts of the city, the use of headphones rather than loudspeakers is being tried out during the 1986 season. The success and popularity of open-top buses in Bath was not fully appreciated when first introduced in 1983; the running of the route in 1986 requires 4 buses on the Scenic Tour and one, usually 8600, on the Heritage Tour. To meet this, three 2-door VRTs (numbered 5033, 5034 and 5035) were converted to permanent open-top with the centre doorway removed in time for the 1985 timetable and renumbered 8615, 8616 and 8617 (JHW 107 - 109P) in the open-top series.

It is interesting to note that the roofs of convertible buses operating in Bath and Weston-Super-Mare are removed from the vehicles at Kensington Depot, Bath and stored there until they are replaced at the end of the Summer. The mind boggles at future developments of the tourist market but has anyone heard of open-top minibuses?

*The fact that it was a two-door bus is given away by the blank stair panel half way along the lower saloon on 8615 (JHW 107P). The BATH fleetname positions are well illustrated and the BH depot allocation plate fixed to all Bath vehicles can be seen. Despite the poor weather it is carrying a good passenger load. (Stephen White)*

# CHAPTER 6 – "WE'RE NOT ON SERVICE!"
## (TRAINING BUSES)

Bus companies have always used old buses to train recruits to PSV standards and the Bath companies have been no exception. The only new vehicles that have been used for training purposes are the Ford Transit minibuses which have been used for driver training since January 1986. This has happened because drivers of minibuses only require a Class 4 PSV licence. When insufficient minibuses have been available for this purpose, similar Fords have been hired from other National Bus Companies such as Southern National and Alder Valley South.

Vehicles such as Bristol VRTs or RELLs, Metrobuses and Leyland Nationals have been used for driver familiarisation when they were first introduced into the fleets. Drivers were usually allowed an hour or so to acquaint themselves with the different cab layouts, gears and controls with an Instructor, before the buses entered revenue-earning service.

Many districts in Bath have been used to train recruits and the crunch of a missed gear selection on a crash gearbox bus was usually caused by a novice under instruction rather than an experienced PSV driver on a service journey, although this has not always been the case!

Double-deck buses have long been the preferred vehicle for tuition work to enable candidates to obtain a PSV "All Types" or Class 1 licence, although, occasionally, withdrawn single-deckers have been adapted. The current Bath training vehicle is W177 (530 OHU) which is a Bristol FLF fitted with a Gardner 6LW engine. It was built in 1963, originally carried fleet number 7087, and was normally allocated to Marlborough Street Bus Station in Bristol. When required, W177 is assisted by another FLF6G training bus allocated to Weston-super-Mare but more recently usually garaged at Marlborough Street. An influx

*W83 (GL 6615) was originally 2250 in the Bath Tramways Motor Co fleet and was received in May 1939. In April 1942 it received perimeter seating for 30 passengers and was renumbered V2250 (the V standing for victory) but reverted to normal seating arrangements for 32 in November 1945, losing the V prefix at the same time. The body was reconstructed sometime between 1945 and 1951. A Bristol L5G, it was selected for use as a Driver Training Vehicle and was operated on these duties between January 1955 and November 1956 when it was withdrawn and sold to a showman. It was captured by the camera at Down Lane in Bathampton on 14th November 1955. (P.R. Forsey)*

*W79 (GL 6602) was a Bristol K5G with Bristol 56-seat body. Originally numbered 3801 in the Bath Electric Tramways fleet, it was purchased in May 1939 for tram replacement and transferred to tuition duties in August 1954. It is seen in Great Pulteney Street on 10th March 1955. (P.R. Forsey)*

of driving trainees led to the hiring, from Southdown Motor Services in Brighton, of a Leyland PD3 registered HCD364E with fully fronted Northern Counties bodywork, in order to clear the training programme in March and April 1985. The bus was suitable to train staff for an "All Types" PSV licence but, unlike the FLFs, possessed a preselect gearbox. The bus was finished in a yellow and white livery used by Southdown on their training buses.

The FLF trainers were adapted for use as driver training units by the removal of the front staircase, removal of the rear bulkhead in the cab and the fitting of a window in place of the advertising panel immediately to the rear of the cab door. The Instructor sits immediately behind the trainee in a position which allows him to keep a watchful eye on all that is going on and to intervene if the situation demands! Because there are few manual gearbox buses, except minibuses, in many fleets, operators now train recruits to Class 1A standards so that the employee is licensed to drive any type of bus provided that it is fitted with either semi-automatic or fully automatic transmission.

In the 1950s and 1960s training buses were difficult to distinguish from service buses as they were all painted in the same Tilling green livery except that the training buses had an additional thick orange band painted below the lower deck windows. To passengers there appeared to be no difference and they regularly attempted to board when the bus pulled onto a bus stop. This could be extremely embarrassing when trainee conductors were also on board for their tuition as they earnestly attempted to convince hopeful passengers that the bus really was not on service! The author has vivid memories of being in this situation in 1978 at Snow Hill near Kensington Depot. These problems have been slightly improved with the use of front entrance vehicles with power operated doors rather than the open, rear platform buses.

In an attempt to make training buses stand out to passengers; they were repainted all over cream with an orange band below the lower deck windows during the 1970s but even this did not always deter the ever enthusiastic public who still attempted to board. The latest livery is dark blue with no relief but large red lettering between decks proclaiming driver training vehicle in capitals and the warning "Caution – Driver Under Instruction" in the space previously occupied by the destination box at the front and below the lower deck windows at the rear.

Badgerline currently has one full time Instructor

*W127 (OHY 938) was a Bristol KSW6B with lowbridge body by ECW incorporating the sunken upper-deck gangway on the offside and four abreast seating. It was new to Bath Tramways Motor Co in September 1952 and was usually to be seen on country routes. It became a tuition bus in October 1967 and was bought by Peter Davey of Bristol for preservation in April 1974. It is pictured here, however, in the cream and orange training livery of the 1970s. (R.F. Mack)*

at Bath who is assisted, when required, by two part-time driving Instructors and an Inspector who was previously an Instructor, all of whom are based at Bath. Extra assistance has been required, particularly during recruitment for minibus staff, and this has been supplied by both Marlborough Street in Bristol and Weston-super-Mare, who have part-time Instructors who return to driving duties when not instructing.

Ticket machine instruction is also given to employees in the classroom from a driver who has been selected especially for this purpose, before he takes them out on the road and supervises them for a few days whilst they take fares and deal with the passengers.

Training people for PSV work is not cheap but the Company is now, more than ever, eager to ensure that the driver is right for the passengers in all ways.

*W162 (989 EHW) is seen in the latest training bus livery at Kensington Depot. It was a Bristol LD6G with ECW 58-seat body incorporating platform doors. It was delivered to Bath Tramways Motor Co in October 1959 and was released for tuition work in September 1976. It was finally sold in February 1979 and eventually went to a Yorkshire dealer in August 1981. It carried fleet number L8537. (C.W. Routh)*

*When Bristol Omnibus took over the services in the Chippenham and Trowbridge areas operated by Western National, a number of buses were also taken into the Bristol fleet. One was Bristol FLF6B 7317 (820 KDV) seen here on 2nd August 1975 operating a Chippenham town service. This bus was later transferred to Bath along with all the other ex-WN FLFs and operated on Bath city and country routes. The author well remembers getting wet sleeves when changing the front destination blinds as a conductor! (D.G. Ormiston)*

*7297 (JHW 65E) was new to Bristol City fleet as C7297 on 1st January 1967. It was a Bristol FLF6B and was captured operating Service 203 on 5th March 1979. Unlike Bath buses, the Bristol City FLFs had extremely loud bells. It was transferred to Bath on 1st March 1979, withdrawn from service in 1980 and sold for scrap in February 1981. Note the absence of Cave-Brown-Cave radiators either side of the destination box and the fitting of only a three track numeral box instead of four tracks on Bath's examples. (A.R. Macfarlane)*

New vehicles have occasionally been loaned by other operators and depots to ease the availability of suitable buses or coaches for service. Secondhand vehicles have also been purchased at times to meet service revision demands for specific vehicle types, particularly following the results of the Market Analysis Project surveys (MAP) in 1979 which increased the requirement for double-deckers on Bath city services.

Various sources have been tapped for the supply of suitable buses but since the formation of the National Bus Company, the needs of the member companies and vehicles surplus to requirements have been regularly circulated. This has often led to buses, particularly double-deckers, being transferred from one area of the country to another.

During 1980 and 1981, the whole fleet of 15 highbridge 74-seat ECW-bodied Bristol VRTs, which were new to London Country Bus Services in 1977, was transferred to Bristol Omnibus Company. It was originally intended to allocate all these vehicles to Bath depot for use on Bath city services and the routes between Bath and Bristol. Due to the height of the bodywork these buses could not be used on the routes between Bath and Trowbridge, Salisbury via Devizes or Warminster, severely restricting their availability for service. In the end only 4 of the VRTs were allocated to Bath carrying fleet numbers 6501 (PPH 462R) now renumbered 6516, 6504 (PPH 465R), 6509 (PPH 470R) and 6514 (PPH 475R). These buses were originally equipped with Leyland 501 engines but all vehicles in the batch are being re-engined with Gardner 6LXB units.

*8608 (UFX 860S) was new to Hants and Dorset in 1977 who later sold it to Southern Vectis. In 1983 Bristol Omnibus purchased two convertible open-top VRTs from Southern Vectis for service at Weston. Still wearing Weston and Wells local identity fleetnames it was caught on Service 11 to Whiteway on 2nd December 1983. (S.M. Chislett)*

*Highbridge buses were uncommon at Bath until the arrival of the Metrobuses and ex-London Country VRTs which were purchased in 1980 and 1981. All 15 VRTs owned by LCBS were bought and it was originally intended to allocate them all to Bath. Thoughts changed and eventually four were sent to Bath. 6509 (PPH 470R) was new in 1977 and is pictured on Service 203 from Bathford at Parade Gardens on 9th September 1982 and shows a broadside advertisement and clear Bristol fleetname. It was BT10 in the LCBS fleet. (A.R. Macfarlane)*

Other double-deck buses purchased from other NBC companies and allocated to Bath are 5600-5602 (JNU 136-138N) which are Series 2 Bristol VRTs with 70-seat lowbridge ECW bodies and Gardner engines. They were new to East Midland Motor Services in 1975 and transferred to Bath in 1982. A further VRT, but a Series 3 model with 74-seat ECW bodywork, was obtained from West Riding Automobile in 1983. Registered MUA874P, it was given fleet number 5615.

Various coaches and dual purpose vehicles suitable for stage carriage or coaching work have been purchased. Eight Bristol RELHs were bought from Eastern National in February 1985, 3 of which were sent to Bath. They were equipped with Gardner 6HLX engines, 51-seat bodies and numbered 2082, 2083 and 2085 (XOO 880L/881L and GJD 195N). These vehicles were not particularly popular with all the drivers and have

recently been transferred to Weston-super-Mare but before leaving Bath were re-registered CSV 231, CSV 303 and CSV 618. All were painted in the Badgerline Swiftlink livery for use on the Company's limited stop services.

A Leyland Leopard PSU3E/4R coach was purchased from National Travel South West in 1983 to assist in the expansion of the Bath coaching fleet. New in 1978 and registered WFH169S, it carries a Plaxton Supreme body with seating for 53 passengers. Two further Leyland Leopards built in 1972 with Plaxton 49-seat bodies were purchased for Bath in 1984 from East Yorkshire Motor Services and allocated fleet numbers 2106 and 2108. Originally registered BKH 921K and BKH 923K they were re-registered VCL 461 and VOP 878, respectively, and have now been withdrawn, registration VCL 461 being allocated to open-top bus 8600.

*3017 (JHW 105P) is an 11.3 metre Leyland National with seating for 52 passengers. It was delivered on 1st August 1975 and was to have been numbered 1476, but it was decided to number single-door and dual-door buses in separate sequences. It is seen operating on Service 218 to Bath University on 9th September 1982 with a Cheltenham fleetname on the nearside. On the offside it carried a Gloucester fleetname! It was sent from the Gloucester and Cheltenham area to Bath on 8th August 1982. (A.R. Macfarlane)*

A really eye-catching vehicle, borrowed from National Travel West in July 1984, was a double-deck coach for use on Service 603 between Bath and London. Registered A117 KBA, it was an impressive three-axled MCW Metroliner finished to National Express Rapide specification and equipped with video screens on both decks, a toilet downstairs and a galley area where drinks and food could be prepared by the hostess when operating on Rapide routes. There was seating for 55 passengers upstairs and 18 downstairs and the vehicle brought many favourable comments from passengers and staff alike, even though a hostess was never carried at Bath!

Vehicle 8600 was delivered new to King Alfred Motor Services of Winchester in 1967. It was a Leyland Atlantean with Roe 74-seat bodywork and was transferred to Hants and Dorset Motor Services when the business was sold. 8600 was purchased from H & D in 1979 and was converted to open-top for use at Weston-super-Mare until it was transferred to Bath to launch the city's open-top service.

During the Second World War certain buses were loaned to the Bath companies by Brighton Hove and District and the London Passenger Transport Board and are detailed in Chapter 3. Bath has also supplied vehicles for other operators, one notable instance being in 1967 when Southern and Western

National were interested in purchasing a number of 60-seat double-deckers. The only new double-deckers available at that time were 70-seaters and the Bristol company offered to sell 20 of their 6-year old FSFs. Included in these were the 3 Bath FSF buses carrying fleet numbers 6008, 6009 and 6041 (704/705 JHY and 806 MHW).

These were replaced at Bath by an influx of Bristol KSWs dating from 1952 which had been allocated to Bristol Joint Services (Bristol City). The KSWs transferred from BJS to Bath Electric Tramways were 8040 (NHY 962) on 1st March 1966 and 8075 (NHY 997) on 1st April 1967. Those transferred to Bath Tramways Motor Company were 8039 (NHY 961) on 1st March 1966; 8071 and 8073 (NHY 993/995 on 1st April 1967; followed by 8070, 8072 and 8074 (NHY 992/994 and 996) and 8082 (OHY 956) on 1st May 1967. These buses were easily recognised as ex-BJS vehicles as they were equipped with a route number box only at the rear and all originally carried a 'C' prefix to their fleet number (e.g. C8039).

The author well remembers seeing, in 1966, a red Bristol RELL, carrying United fleet names, being driven over all Bath city routes to test the suitability of this bus for operation on the routes. The vehicle was at Bath for a few days but was not used on service.

5615 (MUA 874P) is a 1975 Series 3 Bristol VRT with 74-seat ECW body. It was purchased from West Riding Automobile Co in 1983. It is seen here operating on Service 11 to Whiteway on 17th March 1984. It was numbered 752 in the West Riding fleet. (M.S. Curtis)

*Extensive damage occurred to trams 18 and 6 when they collided on Wells Road on 3rd July 1933. Two passengers were killed when number 6 slipped on tar on the line at Hayesfield Park while climbing the hill. The motorman was unable to prevent the tram from rolling backwards as the brake blocks were covered in tar. The damaged trams are seen at the bottom of Wells Road. (A. Gallop collection)*

*2292 (LHY 966) is in a particularly difficult situation on Limpley Stoke Hill on 14th January 1954. It was operating Service 53 from Bath to Warminster when it became stuck on ice. It is a Bristol L5G with ECW 53-seat rear-entrance body. (P.R. Forsey)*

*Fred Dark, Bath's Traffic Superintendent, is seen here using a clothes line prop to raise telephone wires at Elmhurst Estate when route testing the roads with KSW6B 8101 (OHY 950), photographed on 2nd April 1956. Following this test, a service from the estate was introduced on 9th April 1956. (P.R. Forsey)*

*L8516 (970 EHW) was extensively damaged by a falling tree during a storm at Corsham in May 1975. Tragically the driver, Ray Cormack, was killed in the accident. The remains were sold as scrap in December that year. (Bristol Vintage Bus Group)*

*...ooding used to be quite a common occurrence until the Bath flood prevention scheme was completed. On 4th December 1960 KSW6B (NHY 951) is seen battling through flood ...ter at Stambridge on its way to Elmhurst Estate on Service 3A. The blind has already been set for the return journey. (P.R. Forsey)*

*Opposite:*
*VRT SL6G 5507 (KOU 793P) had been painted as an overall advertisement for the Great American Disaster restaurant and became a disaster itself when it caught fire on Saturday 23rd July 1983. It had been repainted in fleet livery when this happened just inside the Avon boundary at Shockerwick Bridge while operating to Bath. Fortunately there were no casualties although the bus was a write-off. (Badgerline Ltd)*

*26th July 1956, KSW6B 8032 (NHY 954) lost control on steep Bathford Hill, crashed through a wall and overturned. The seven passengers were not injured but the bus was ... ly damaged on the nearside. (Reproduced by courtesy of Bath Evening Chronicle)*

A company operating more than a handful of vehicles requires an efficient maintenance department to provide the essential facilities which allow these vehicles onto the road in a safe and roadworthy state. Stringent standards of vehicle maintenance set by the Department of Transport have to be met and regular servicing and vehicle checks are carried out by the maintenance department at Kensington Depot to achieve this. Most accident repairs, repaints and unit changes can be carried out at Bath although major body rebuilds sometimes have to be contracted out, particularly when there is pressure on space in the body or unit shops.

Inevitably major accident damage does occasionally occur and a breakdown wagon suitable for retrieving vehicles as large as a double-deck bus, has long been stationed at Bath. The area around the city is fortunate in that it is not renowned to suffer too much from adverse weather conditions. It is not unknown, though, for heavy snow, flooding, high winds or severe frost to take its toll and disrupt the service, much to the annoyance of the passengers. Every endeavour, however, is made by the maintenance and traffic departments to restore the scheduled services as soon as possible when the conditions are trying their utmost to prevent this! Quite often a breakdown call is received by an Engineering Supervisor or Traffic Inspector just after the breakdown crew have left the depot to attend another breakdown, most probably in completely the opposite direction. The current Badgerline breakdown vehicles based at Bath are an unusual 3-axled Magirus Deutz, capable of righting an overturned double-deck bus, and a 3-axled Leyland Bison which was previously a petroleum tanker.

Many of the traditional craftsman skills are still required and buses are hand painted rather than sprayed although advertisements on bus exteriors are now generally printed on self adhesive vinyls rather than hand painted by a signwriter. An automatic bus wash has been a feature of Kensington Depot for many years and is a great advance on the hosepipes and extremely long-handled brushes of the past.

*Breakdowns and accidents are an inevitable occurrence where a large number of vehicles are operated. Carrying trade plates 525 HT, this AEC Matador first entered service with Bristol Omnibus in September 1966 and continued until 1985 when it was replaced by a Magirus Deutz. The livery in this photograph is orange and cream. It was nicknamed Jumbo. (Badgerline Ltd)*

This impressive looking vehicle replaced Jumbo at Bath and is a Magirus Deutz Uranus six-wheel drive, weighing almost 18½ tons with a maximum speed of 31 mph and is capable of a winch pull of 78,400 lbs. The design is based on the Swiss Army version which was required to pull tanks over the Alps! (Badgerline Ltd)

Originally Bristol LH6L bus 373 (KHU 323P) carrying an ECW 43-seat body, by the time that this picture was taken it had been converted into a light towing vehicle using trade plates 031 FB. As a bus it was new in 1976 and was converted by Garage Engineer Ken Horler with maintenance employees R. Dyte, R. Millard, E. Hulbert, S. Brown, T. Fletcher and R. Bland. It was finished in a yellow livery and carried a red BATH fleetname and NBC logo. It has since been transferred to Marlborough Street Bus Station in Bristol. (Badgerline Ltd)

An early overall advertisement bus was VRT 5507 (KOU 793P) painted to the requirements of a Bath restaurant which did not remain open for long! It is seen on Service 213 to Foxhill Estate. (Bristol Vintage Bus Group)

6509 (PPH 470R) is the only ex-London Country highbridge VRT to have carried an overall or Colorbus advertisement for a considerable time. It was caught operating Service 3 to Bathford after it had been loaned to Bristol Bus Station for operation on their services at the request of the advertiser. The date is 4th July 1984 and in August 1986 the bus still retained this livery. (S.M. Chislett)

The broadside style of advertisement is displayed by Auto-VRT 5536 (EWS 744W) at Parade Gardens on 3rd October 1984. It was new on 23rd August 1981. (A.R. Macfarlane)

A Marlborough Street Auto-VRT, Number 5544 (EWS 752W), advertises Canon equipment on a 'Unibus' advertisement at Bath Bus Station in August 1983. (S.M. Chislett)

# ADVERTISEMENTS

*5541 (EWS 749W) is seen in Railway Street carrying a 'Unibus' advertisement between the decks. Note the absence of the NBC logo. It was photographed in July 1985. (S.M. Chislett)*

*The Metrobuses were all delivered in special liveries to advertise fare offers available on the company's services. 6001 (DAE 511W) is seen crossing Churchill Bridge on 21st February 1981 wearing a yellow and blue colour scheme to advertise Rovercards. It is operating to Foxhill Estate and not Elmhurst Estate! (M.S. Curtis)*

*Bristol Bus Station does not have chassis cleaning facilities and this work is normally carried out at Bath's Kensington Depot. The bus involved is then usually allocated to a Bath city service until it can be transferred back onto a Bristol crew working. 9506 (JHU 905X), a Leyland Olympian with Roe body, is seen operating Service 12 to Whiteway in July 1985 in Dorchester Street. (S.M. Chislett)*

*The Eagle Star broadside advertisement, incorporating an eagle whose wings cover parts of the upper-deck windows, has been applied to buses throughout the country. VRT 5510 (KOU 796P) was selected at Bath for this purpose as it was the only VRT still in pre-Badgerline livery at the time. It is seen in Railway street on Service 3 to Bathford in June 1986. (S.M. Chislett)*

3757 (LAE 716), a Bristol K5G of 1948, shows the three-line single-unit display used immediately following the Second World War. It is seen leaving the Guildhall. (Peter G. Davey)

MW5G 2956 stands alongside LS5G 2929 at Bath Bus Station. The MW is fitted with the BOC T type destination box with separate four-track numeral equipment. The LS carries the one-piece destination screen which often resulted in stickers giving service information being displayed in the windscreen if not contained on the blind. The T type box at least allowed the service number to be displayed. (Bristol Vintage Bus Group)

Only two buses based at Bath are fitted with Transign destination equipment. They are 5545 and 5546 both of which are Auto-VRTs. 5545 was caught at Elmhurst Estate on 10th April 1983 when operating from Bathford to Foxhill Estate on Service 23. (S.M. Chislett)

Tin bible metal destination displays were specified by Bath Tramways in the late 1930s even though roller blinds were common elsewhere. 2218 (GL 5056) is pictured on service to Trowbridge during September 1942 in wartime livery. (S.L. Poole, courtesy London Bus Preservation Group)

*Still carrying Gloucester fleetnames FLF6G, G7233 (EHT 855C) also still carries the G prefix to the fleetnumber. Note that the rear destination box has been panelled over to provide additional advertising space. (Bristol Vintage Bus Group)*

*KSW6G 8268 was owned by Bath Tramways Motor Co and is seen at Bristol Bus Station. It shows the later reduced version of the single-piece destination display very well. (Bristol Vintage Bus Group)*

*As part of uniform issue, drivers and conductors were expected to wear a scroll badge of the company's initials. Bath Electric Tramways Ltd's scroll is seen here. (S.M. Chislett)*

*The Bath Services fleetname is displayed on 7216. (Bristol Vintage Bus Group/D. Withers)*

# PEOPLE

*Stan Weston is seen in his conductor's uniform with driver Jack Bolton of Market Lavington. They were photographed in 1928 at Tinhead, now absorbed into the village of Edington, while operating on the Market Lavington to Trowbridge route. (Stan Weston)*

*The 1925 team of the Kensington Garage AFC proudly pose for the photographer in the depot yard. (Jack Bishop collection)*

# PEOPLE

The basic structure of Straker Squire double deck bus FB-011 can be clearly seen in this photograph taken in Market Lavington in about 1913. Mr. B. Sayer is driving with Mrs. Sayer and their son Fred sat alongside and Mr. Sayer's own mother occupying the nearside seat. The lamps on the stanchion are of interest. (Stan Weston)

Lavington and Devizes Motor Services garage was situated in the Market Place in Market Lavington. Mr. Sayer, the proprietor, is seen standing next to his wife and John Cooper the blacksmith. Jaky the dog, Harry Hobbs, George Hobbs and Charlie Sheppard complete the line up outside the garage in about 1923. (Stan Weston)

# PARAPHERNALIA

*The Bell Punch Company supplied ticket equipment to many tramway and bus undertakings throughout the country including Bath Tramways. These were replaced by Setright machines for conductors during the early 1950s and were later adapted for use with electric motors on one man buses. In May 1986 the Setright equipment was replaced by Wayfarer electronic ticket machines at Bath. The Bell Punch required the conductor to punch prepriced tickets which were carried in a rack made of either metal or wood. Conductors operating on the Salisbury runs used exceptionally large racks and waybills due to the length of the journey and consequential large number of ticket values. The Bell Punch and rack were both kindly loaned by Stan Weston. (S.M. Chislett)*

*Bath Electric Tramways issued certain staff with leather bound passes which were bottle green in colour. This one was kindly loaned by Stan Weston and was originally issued on 19th January 1931 to Mr. Sayer, proprietor of Lavington and Devizes Motor Services. (S.M. Chislett)*

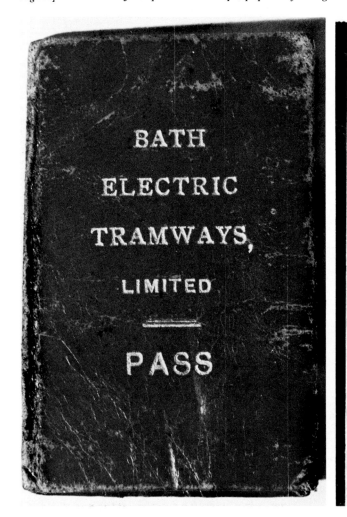

No. 6·15    Issued 19 JAN 1931

*Mr. Sayer*

IS ENTITLED
to travel over any portion of the TRAMWAY or OMNIBUS ROUTES subject to the Company's Bye-Laws.

This Pass must be shown to the Conductors or Inspectors upon demand, and should only be used by the person to whom it is assigned.

**E. H. R. TRENOW,**
*Managing Director.*

1392 900 12 30

*When Bristol Tramways began running taxis in Bath, signs were erected at various locations to advertise the facility. The plate was loaned by Lionel Tancock for copying. (S.M. Chislett)*

*In the 1950s, buses carried farecharts in the saloon. The one here is dated 28th April 1957 and gives all fares applicable for Bath City Services at the time. (S.M. Chislett)*

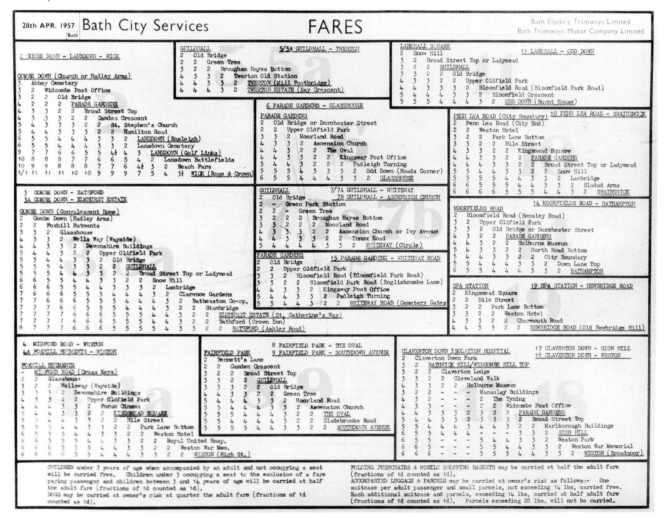

# TAILPIECE

*Carrying its second body, but its first at Bath, 3822 (DKN 39) stands outside the Abbey on Service 7A to Whiteway (Circle) via Old Bridge and Ascension Church. The camber of the road gives the view an unsteady feeling. (Bristol Vintage Bus Group)*

*It doesn't add up? The road sign says "road up" as Bristol K5G 3840 passes the work in Southgate Street on 1st February 1958. (P.R. Forsey)*

# TAILPIECE

The small rear destination display is unused on 2250 (GL 6615), a Bristol L5G, captured at Grand Parade on 10th February 1954. The central emergency exit is very similar to those on the bodies of the Bristol RE type buses introduced from 1967. (Peter G. Davey)

2012 (971 DAE) was new in December 1958 and given fleet number 2951 in June 1966. It is seen here in Railway Street proudly boasting that it is a Bath Services vehicle. It is finished in the dual purpose livery of the time. The date of the shot is 1966. (A.R. Macfarlane)

Bristol L5G 2475 (MHW 986) was a one man operated bus when photographed on 25th March 1958. It had previously been C2754 in the Bristol City fleet. (P.R. Forsey)

# POSTSCRIPT

The full implementation of the 1985 Transport Act on 26th October 1986 will mark a further milestone and major change in bus operation. On that date bus services will be deregulated so that routes will no longer require individual licences although 42 days notice will have to be given to the local authorities and Traffic Commissioners indicating notice of intention to introduce, alter or withdraw services. Operators of stage carriage services and coaching activities will continue to require an Operator's Licence, however, and drivers will also need to possess a PSV Licence. The full effects of the Act on local transport are not known at the time of writing and will only become fully apparent during 1987. It is difficult to say whether the aim of the Conservative Government in implementing the Act, to bring in competition on bus services, will be achieved in Bath. Badgerline has converted many city services to minibus operation often resulting in frequencies as high as every 3 to 4 minutes on some routes which had previously run hourly or half-hourly with standard style buses. The initial changes involved five services on Sunday 16th February 1986 followed on Sunday 27th and Monday 28th April by another three routes. The 28th April changes also introduced minibuses to areas never served by buses before, on the number 16 route between the Bus Station and Kingsway.

From this date the frequencies of standard bus routes 5, between the Bus Station and the Twerton and Whiteway housing estates, and 10 and 11, between the city centre and Southdown, were also improved. On Sunday 18th May routes serving the Weston area of the city were transferred to minibus operation. The opportunity was also taken to expand coverage of Weston by using roads which had been considered unsuitable for use by standard buses. These conversions allowed a number of drivers to take voluntary redundancy but have not resulted in any compulsory redundancies. Other services which remain double-deck or single-deck have or will be increased in frequency although the success of minibuses could alter plans. The effects of deregulation have resulted in the Company submitting a commercial network of time-tables, run without subsidy from local or central government, with many services losing evening and Sunday journeys when it is not profitable to provide the service at those times. The Company may still be running journeys after 26th October on unprofitable services if the tenders offered by the Company are accepted by the local authorities.

The bold liveries and name of the new Company, marketed under the Minilink name, are well accepted by passengers and staff and it is sometimes difficult to remember Bath before Badgerline! The high frequency of service offered by minibuses has, without doubt, encouraged an increase in patronage. It is very difficult to predict the future style of bus operation but there is no doubt that it will be interesting to say the least!